INTERVIEW RULE BOOK

FIRST EDITION

Mike Zolin & Rob Christensen
Published by TopScore
INTERVIEWRULEBOOK.COM

ISBN-13: 978-0996127134

Thanks to our editors, Erika Heeren and Andria Wallace.

This book is brought to you by TopScore and www.interview911.com.

FORWARD

As the job landscape continues to shift, there has never been a more important time to have a clearly defined game plan while conducting a job search. Just as no fire fighter would enter a home to battle a blaze without a plan of attack, no job seeker should enter the market without a strategy to battle employment.

I've spent nearly 20 years as the Chief Operations Officer of a talent acquisition firm and my professional career has been dedicated to teaching and coaching interview tactics and strategies. What I have spent a professional lifetime verbalizing to my clients, has finally seen pen put to paper with "The Interview Rule Book". This book represents what I have spent a lifetime verbalizing to my clients.

For years, the interview process has been one-sided. The power of the interview has been held and wielded by those hiring, while those on the other side of the table have been left guessing and grasping at straws.

The game changes NOW!

"The Interview Rule Book" is not only a guide on how to land your dream job, but it is a comprehensive step-by-step look into the interview and hiring process. The insights shared in this book clearly define a strategy to take the power of the interview and for the first time, put that power back into the hands of those interviewing.

As the path of employment continues to change and evolve, so too do the tactics needed to constantly stay one step ahead. With the old model and outdated rules finding themselves thrown out the window, it is "The Interview

Rule Book" that stands poised to be the catalyst for career change.

With a dream career just a successful interview away, it's time to better prepare yourself for the future you deserve. "The Interview Rule Book" is a game changing interview weapon for those that are serious about achieving and succeeding in the constantly evolving modern employment market and is the first step by step guideline on how to identify and acquire your dream job.

Josh Bear

Chief Operations Office

Jivaro Professional Headhunters

TABLE OF CONTENTS

INTRODUCTION

Today's job market is extremely competitive. Whether you are looking to obtain your first job, making a career change, interviewing for college admission, or seeking a promotion, you will find that the *Interview Rule Book* is unlike any other interview book available. This book will *not* give you answers to 100 different interview questions. If we answered all of the questions for you, the answers would not be ***you***. We want you to stand out!

This book has the tools to provide winning answers for any interview by using a framework consisting of three elements; 1) a five-step process for answering questions called the **TopScore Top5**, 2) a way to personalize your assets using **Marketing Priorities**, and 3) a way to incorporate your values into your job target using **Core Values**. Throughout these three elements are **The Rules**. Let's look at the elements in detail.

TopScore Top5 are the five things you need to include when answering interview questions about you and your life experiences. These include a personal history, a personal story, company knowledge, and keywords.

Marketing Priorities are highlights from your life that contribute to uniquely personalized answers. Marketing Priorities are the things you want the oral board or interviewer to know about you. Some, but not all of these priorities can be gathered from your resume. If, for example, when you were sixteen years old and the first person on location of a car accident, you quickly assessed the situation and assisted by using first aid techniques you learned in health class. The fire department complimented you on the great job you did, which inspired you to become a firefighter. Using that story in your TopScore answer makes you stand out.

Core Values can be defined as the fundamental beliefs of a person or an organization. Core values are the guiding principles that dictate your behavior and actions. Knowing and defining your Core Values will help you answer questions to show how your Core Values contribute to any position.

The Rules. Why do we call our instructions a rulebook? There are many rules to follow when interviewing for a job or a promotion. Most of these rules are unspoken. We have established **The Rules** through years of interviews, coaching and feedback from our students. We have seen candidates fail because they did not know **The Rules**. We have learned what interviewers are looking for in a great answer. We are going to show you these previously hidden gems that will improve your answers, and your overall "score" dramatically. Not knowing the rules can make the difference between being hired and continuing on the job interview circuit. We also understand the time and expense involved in trying to obtain employment; we have been there. Our goal is to help you cut down the amount of time, energy, and expense involved in your pursuit of a career.

The Workbook: You will have homework to do and our comprehensive workbook will help you keep it organized. In the workbook, you'll find sections to help you detail your Personal History, Personal Story, Key Words, Company Knowledge, Marketing Priorities, Core Values, Interpersonal Skills, Teamwork, Communication Skills, Professional Development, Diversity and Customer Service Skills.

You'll also find:

- A sample interview sheet
- TopScore mock interview scorecards
- Interview questions
- Ride-along form
- A follow-up form to track your progress
- "After Your Interview" forms
- TopScore 3x5 card method of study
- Background information page

One of the great aspects of our book is that it is co-authored. This means it contains two different points of view and two different styles of teaching. One author's style of teaching is linear and the other is more creative. We were able to mesh them into this one-of-a-kind comprehensive book. Whatever style suits your personality, we have it covered.

Let's get started!

Getting Started

Mindset: Power of Positive Thinking

When I was first on the fire testing circuit, my brother gave me a small booklet titled "The Power of Positive Thinking" by Norman Vincent Peale. "It actually works," he added. He was right! This small booklet would provide valuable guidance to new life habits that have been at the core of my success.

Consider the following advice from Norman Vincent Peale:

> *"Anybody can do just about anything with himself that he really wants to and makes up his mind to do. We are all capable of greater things than we realize."*
>
> *"Formulate and stamp indelibly on your mind a mental picture of yourself as succeeding. Hold this picture tenaciously. Never permit it to fade. Your mind will seek to develop the picture."*
>
> *"Believe it is possible to solve your problem. Tremendous things happen to the believer. So believe the answer will come. It will."*
>
> *"Your thoughts will become your beliefs, and your beliefs become who you are."*

Having a positive mindset throughout the hiring process, I could eliminate negative self-talk, while also reducing stress. If you are not an optimistic person, this is your notice for change, and be patient as this will take practice. Optimism is a key part to affect stress management.

Though positive thinking, along with the teachings of this book, you will succeed. Make positive thinking a part of your daily routine.

THE APPLICATION PROCESS

Before we discuss the interview, let's take a few minutes to describe the process that comes before applying for the job.

With the advent of the computer, this process has changed a lot from years past. Very few jobs use paper applications You need to approach a business or organization prepared.

Have your resume ready. Many employers, even those hiring for entry-level positions, will ask for a resume. You need to make sure that you have one ready. There are numerous examples of resumes out there, just make sure that yours is easy to read and completely free of errors. If you have never had a job, you may not have work experience to detail in your resume. That's okay, show your experience through school activities, clubs you belong to, and special classes you are taking in school. Anything that you participate in can be a valuable asset to you.

Some employers rely solely on resumes for their hiring selection process. You'll need to prepare for this, and have your resume ready to submit in whatever form they require, including paper, and a digital copy on a thumb drive, including references and cover letter. Sometimes, they will have a form online, or they will give you an email address to send it to. If they give you an email address, make sure you include a cover letter in the body of your email. Don't forget, you are doing what you can to impress a possible future employer. Be professional. It is a good idea to have a professional email address. Make sure everything is spelled correctly and is easy to read. Be sure at least two people review it to catch any errors you might have missed. Your resume is likely their first impression of you. If it is not a good first impression, they will look elsewhere.

A lot of businesses will ask for both a resume and an online application. This may seem a bit redundant because they both have the same information, but it is important to follow their directions exactly. Make sure you fill out the online application completely and with as much detail as your resume, since some systems create a resume using the online information.

It is not uncommon for an employer to stop you when you turn in an application and ask you if you had a few minutes to talk. Should this happen, don't say no! They are looking for reasons to hire you, or reject your application. Give them every reason to put you on the top of their list!

After you put in an application, online or in person, wait a few days and then contact the employer. This is important, particularly if there may be a lot of people vying for the position. This way, they know that you are interested, and the extra effort may make the hiring manager notice of your application more than your competitors.

An employer may call you unexpectedly and ask you if you have a few minutes for a quick screening/pre-interview. Once again, don't say no! Talk to them and give them reason to keep your resume at the top of the stack. If a company can catch you off guard (in their minds) and you still shine like a diamond, it can put you in their number one spot for hire.

The Phone Interview

The phone interview has become more popular in the recent years. It's simply more convenient for the employer to do an initial screening over the phone. Many times, this will provide them with enough information to either move you on to an in-person interview, or reject your application. The following rules will help you prepare for any phone interview:

Rule: Speak slowly and enunciate.

Rule: Smile while you talk. They will hear the smile in your voice. It will also make you feel more confident, and your interviewer will sense that confidence.

Rule: Find a quiet place without any background noise for your interview.

Rule: Use the fill-in pages in this book and have them in front of you for quick reference.

Rule: Get cleaned up and dress professionally. This is important, even for a phone interview. The more professional you look, the better you will feel, and the more confident you will sound in your interview.

Rule: Have a pen and paper ready to write down information. Be certain when writing your notes that you are not doing so in the direct area of your phone's mic as it might transmit the sound.

Rule: Set your phone on a table in front of you on speaker mode. This will prevent "phone drift." Some people have a bad habit of continually moving the mic of their phone down away from their mouth, causing the volume of their voice to come and go. Using ear buds with a mic is acceptable as long as you don't have nervous habit of playing with the wires near the mic.

Rule: Have enthusiasm in your voice. During the first part of the conversation, share your excitement of the possible employment opportunity.

Rule: Have a glass of water nearby to help with the dry mouth that bad nerves can cause. Be conscious of any sound being made when setting your cup or glass down on the surface. A simple placemat or coaster may come in handy.

Rule: Keep the company's strategic plan, recent news, as well as the job description of the job you are applying for available as reference material.

Rule: Have a laptop or pad on you to use for quick reference if you are asked something you may not be familiar with within the company. Remember to turn off all audio alerts.

Rule: As soon as possible, follow up with a *thank-you* note. A hand-written note is key, anyone can send an email, but a personal note stands out. Ensure you have exact spelling/title of the interviewer.

Rule: Record the interview. This information is a great tool and will help you improve in the future.

Rule: Have your planner or calendar in front of you to make for easy scheduling if you should get invited for a face-to-face interview.

Rule: Turn off any alerts to your phone and computer. Do this for both vibration and sound mode.

The Video / over the Internet Interview

Some companies prefer to do a screening interview over the internet. You will need to have a fast internet connection, if you can't rely on one at home, find a quiet place in an office or at a friend's. Have a backdrop so there is nothing distracting. Set up good lighting and buy a microphone. Have the camera at eye level. Make sure there will be no distractions: close the door, put the dog out, send the kids to play at their friends, whatever you need to do to achieve silence. Look at your camera, not at the screen. Once everything is setup just right, do some practice interviews on Skype or Google Hangouts with a friend or family member. Be mindful not to try to fill space by talking, allow for pauses to give yourself time to think of answers, and avoid saying "um". Keep it professional, say "yes" not "yeah", "no" not "nah", and "thank you" instead of "thanks".

Your First Job Interview

As much as education is important in finding a job, the interview skill set is often overlooked in preparing people for the job market.

A first interview is particularly tough since it is a brand new, scary experience. Usually, interviewers want to speak with you about your previous work history. You'll need to explain your previous job or jobs, how you performed, how you worked with others, how you handle conflict, attendance records, and so on. When you have no previous work history, you will need to steer your answers in the line of life experience.

Rule: When you have no employment history, you must rely on life experience. Life experience includes facts about you that provide a clear picture to the interviewer of what they can expect of you as an employee. You *can* and *will* be hired without previous work experience.

Rule: The top traits that employers are looking for in a great employee are not acquired strictly through employment. This "Top Traits" list is applicable for employers looking to fill entry-level to management positions.

Top Traits

1) **Honesty:** If honesty is your way of life, then make certain you share this **TopScore Top Trait** with the interviewer(s).
2) **Strong Work Ethic**: This does not have to stem from a previous job, just how you act in life.
3) **A Teachable and Trainable Spirit:** You learn because you want to, not because you have to.
4) **Dependability:** Telling someone you are going to have a task done by a particular deadline and completing it on or before that deadline. This includes having a great attendance and missing very few days.
5) **Team-Oriented and Mindset:** Enjoy working with others and show that you will always sacrifice for the greater good of the team.
6) **Confident but not cocky:** Having an "air" about oneself. Having a friendly, approachable, winning attitude.

7) **Enthusiastic:** Being excited to be a part of the business and working as part of a team.

8) **Self-Reliant with good problem solving skills:** PAR (Problem, Action, Result)

9) **Good Communication Skills:** As a new employee, your communications skills will be sided with your listening skills.

10) **Conflict Resolution:** Knowing the proper steps in handling conflict.

11) **High Level of Emotional Intelligence:** as determined by Daniel Goleman, author of Emotional Intelligence, *why it can matter more than IQ*, with five main constructs as follows:[i]

    Self-awareness: the ability to know one's emotions, strengths, weaknesses, drives, values and goals and recognizing their impact on others while using gut feelings to guide decisions.

    Self-regulation: involves controlling or redirecting one's disruptive emotions and impulses and adapting to changing circumstances.

    Social skills: managing relationships to move people in the desired direction.

    Empathy: considering other people's feelings, especially when making decisions.

    Motivation: being driven to achieve for the sake of achievement.

What is it that the interviewer(s) needs to know about you that would line up with the person they want to fill a position?

Rule: Do your research on the company and position. You can find information on the company by checking the internet and social media and by talking to employees.

Rule: Talk to recently hired employees to see what the company is looking for.

Whether the job you are trying to attain is your first ever or it is a promotional interview in the middle of your career, the process can be extremely competitive. If you are a competitive person, embrace the process. If you are not, you'll have to motivate yourself to become so. Remember, this job or promotion is something you want!

A company's website is an excellent resource of hiring information. It behooves you as an applying member to check with his or her desired company to ascertain the prerequisites required for the job as well as the general hiring process.

ORAL INTERVIEW

Now we are getting into the bread and butter. If you have made it to an oral interview part of the hiring process, you will need to be exceedingly well prepared. More than likely, there will be a greater number of interviewees than there will be available hiring positions. The interviewer's decision may be made on a candidate's slight screw up or candidate's ability to separate themselves from the rest of the interviewees. This is where your preparation and practice needs to be perfected. This is where the true grit of a candidate is exposed, and it is fiercely competitive.

Look for any and all opportunities to improve yourself. Remember: there could be a fraction of a difference separating you from attaining your dream or facing another day looking through the help wanted ads.

Part of interviewing for a position is salesmanship. You are selling yourself. Salesmanship requires you to show your enthusiasm, passion, positive attitude and compassion. Stay away from negativity or political or religious opinions or prejudices. The art of salesmanship is building and cultivating relationships. When this happens, connecting those "personal history" fishing lines to the interviewer(s) becomes natural, and you are guaranteed to have a more favorable interview, score or connection. The more lines in the water, the better your chances of catching something.

You must accept and perfect the art of selling yourself. No one is going to shout out your accomplishments from the top of a mountain or campaign to the interviewer or hiring board about what a phenomenal asset you will be for the company except for you. The most successful salespeople are individuals who wholeheartedly believe in the product they are selling. This means you need to believe, to your core, that you are the best investment to the company for whom you are interviewing. Who better to present an overwhelming positive view of your abilities and capabilities to the interviewer or the interview board than you? When you effectively sell yourself, it will leave no doubt in their eyes that you will be a tremendous asset, not only now, but 20 years into your career. Yes, this is uncomfortable for most individuals, but you must overcome those nagging doubts and prepare yourself to impart a convincing and outstanding presentation. It takes work, lots of work, but we can honestly say it's worth it!

The interviewer will ask a wide range of questions with specific objectives. The interviewers want to get to know you to the best of their ability and identify if you are a good fit for their company. The interviewer is looking for more than just whether you're a person who is easy to get along with or not, they also want to know if they can depend on you. You need to know and understand that you are interviewing to be part of a family– their family. Always speak from your heart and stay positive and focused on your successes in life. You have only one sale that counts: You.

INTERVIEW PREPARATION

From our experience sitting on numerous interview boards, it is evident if a candidate spent any time at all preparing for their interview. It is as evident as someone trying to play a song on a piano without any previous instruction. By the third keystroke, it is clear the person has no clue what they were doing. Interviewing, like learning to play the piano, takes a lot of practice and hours of preparation, and yet, many go into their interview unprepared. There is no such thing as being over-prepared. Yes, there are people who are naturally gifted in memory recall, articulation, self-confidence, and being soft spoken but commanding attention. But even these interviewees cannot be over prepared.

Start by clearly identifying your job search goal. Write it down and post it where you will see it every day. Reading your goal and visualizing your success will keep you motivated. You cannot afford to be average in this process. Interviewers expect you to meet the objectives they set forth in the questions they ask. You are more marketable than you give yourself credit for. We often do not give ourselves the respect and acknowledgement we deserve. Because of this, in many cases, we are our own worst enemies. During an interview, do not downplay your experience, accomplishments or accreditations. For the candidate with very little work history and life experience, we encourage you to dig through your past for any relevant experience for the job. The fact that you delivered pizza for a summer and are now seeking a job with a parcel delivery company can highlight that you are familiar with the city's address breaks, not to mention knowing fifty percent of the streets. Your mother is not going to be standing over your shoulder telling the board how wonderful you are. You need to make it happen. We often minimize our personal experiences in life. Take a deep look at all you have done and brainstorm your history. Dig deep and you will start to recall key skills, experiences, situations, accomplishments, and victories that you have long since forgotten. There can be hundreds of people competing for one position. Make yourself stand above the crowd.

Fact: People who are most prepared for their interview perform the best.

It is not uncommon for people to commit to developing their interview skillset 20+ hours a week, as if it is a part-time job. Plan ahead, it will take personal sacrifice to set yourself up for success.

Rule: Know the job description inside and out. Go as far as getting advice from those currently working in the position. Find out what it is they enjoy and what challenges they have.

LEARN THE JOB DESCRIPTION

An important part of interview preparation is to thoroughly know the job description. It is not only necessary to know the position you are applying for, but also critical to let the board or interviewer know that you clearly understand the expectations set before you. Do not allow TV shows or movies be your impression of the career you are applying for. Many career job descriptions can be similar for a given field. Look for the unique differences in the particular description for the position you are applying for and bring them up in a positive way during your interview.

Rule: Have a strategy. Your strategy is to make certain that you provide a clear picture to the interviewer of how successful you will be in the position.

TopScore Strategy

Talk about the experiences from your past that are in line with job title.

If the interviewer does not hear about your successful experiences showcasing your skills that fit that job position, they will have trouble visualizing you in the position.

For example, if the employer is looking to hire someone who is detail-oriented, able to work under pressure, and who can perform with little supervision, you will need to make certain that you address all of those characteristics during your interview. You will need to be prepared to share personal experiences of being detail-oriented, a time when you were able to work under pressure, and a time you worked without any direct supervision.

Consider: Though a 35-year old will generally have a more life experience than a 20-year old, it is still an opportunity for the 20-year old to answer with true-life experiences. As you know, some of our most important lessons come from Life. In fact, much of what we are taught and learn growing-up shapes us into the employees we become.

Let's say the 35-year-old in the above example is seeking a position as a manager of TopScore Property Management. He may answer a question with something like this:

During my previous 12 years of employment while working for Boardwalk Property Management, I had to read and accept or reject numerous contracts. These contracts had to be extremely detailed, as it was my responsibility to reject any that were too vague or lacking content. As a property management team competing with numerous other property management teams, it was critical that we attained and then maintained the fastest turnaround time in the industry. This was a lot of work under pressure, and it was under these circumstances that I was able to thrive. I have always been trainable and a quick-learner. I was also working on my own with little to no supervision for the majority of time at Boardwalk Property Management.

The 20-year-old on the other hand, may answer questions while interviewing for a job at TopScore City Golf Course. This employer is looking for someone who is detail oriented, able to work under pressure and perform with very little supervision:

Graduating from high school with a 3.0 GPA required me to be extremely detailed in my schoolwork, most importantly in my AP classes. During the school year, I was in school clubs throughout the year, and I also worked part time at King Pizza. With having a very full schedule, I put a lot of pressure on myself scholastically. Raised by parents who believed in letting us children "live and learn from our own consequences," I was never told to do my homework or to study for a particular test. My parents set clear expectations with clear consequences. I performed with little to no parental supervision over my scholastics and maintained a 3.0 GPA throughout school.

Rule: Everyone wants to hire someone who is enjoyable to be around. Make sure you show that you are enjoyable to be around. Do this by being positive, smiling, and being engaging.

Your interviewer or review board could potentially be made up of people that you could be working with 40 hours a week for years to come. If this is the case, they may want to make sure you have a personality and can share a few laughs with them during the interview should the situation allow for it. We are not saying to enter the interview with jokes in hand, but to understand they may want someone who has a sense of humor. They want someone who is enjoyable to be around and to hang out with now and then at the weekend work functions. Don't make them guess or wonder what you will be like as an employee: tell and show them.

Rule: Print off a generic application. Fill it out and keep it in a folder for filling out applications in the future. Learn to speak on duties/skills/accomplishments/volunteer work. This is your basic note-gathering tool for your job interview.

Your First Impression

Rule: Make a good first impression. The interviewer's first impression occurs well before you walk into the interview. No one gets a second chance to make a first impression. Your application and resume should highlight your skills and abilities to form a positive view of you well before they meet you

Your application may not reach those performing the interview, but it still needs to be filled out properly to form a good impression. Have your application proofread before submitting it. A resume, on the other hand, is usually reviewed by the interviewer prior to the interview and can either help or hurt an impression. The resume needs to be professional and should highlight your greatest assets. Print it on high quality paper. Imagine that you are on the panel or you are the interviewer, and you have seen 30 resumes, all on the same white, boring printer paper. Then you get a professional resume on high quality paper. Is it going to stand out? Is it going to show effort and look better than any other resume? If they do not allow you to submit your resume early or you submitted a resume online, bring several quality copies to the interview.

Second Impression

Rule: Make a good second impression. Your second impression begins the as soon as you walk through the door for the interview. You need to enter the room with enthusiasm and confidence, look the interviewer(s) in the eye, smile, and give firm handshakes. A proper entry and introduction will get everything moving in the right direction. Do your best to remember their names, ranks, and job titles. This will also help ensure that your follow-up thank-you cards will reach the correct person. If you cannot remember names then fall back on using Sir and Ma'am.

Wait for the interviewer to invite you to sit. If the chair is twenty feet away from the table, you need to move it closer. Ask before moving it, and don't move it so close to the table that you invade the interviewer's personal space.

Once seated, be aware of your body position and posture. You need to continue displaying confidence and respect. Simple body gestures such as placing your elbows on the table or slouching will send the wrong message. Some studies show that the spoken word accounts for up to 35% of the message we are trying to convey. This means that the remaining 65% percent is communicated nonverbally.

Amy Cuddy, a Social Psychologist and Associate Professor of Business Administration at Harvard Business School was the keynote speaker on body language at the June 2012 TED TALK Convention. Amy spoke about how people are viewed by others, and how they view themselves. She also explains how to change outside perception of yourself through using appropriate body language, stating "your body language shapes who you are,"

Dress Attire

Rule: Dress according to the position.

It is a simple rule to follow. If it is a professional job, dress appropriately. Wear conservative business attire such as a dark colored suit with a white or gray shirt. Belt, tie, dress shoes (clean and polished) and a clean professional hairstyle. Cologne is a no-go. Too many people have allergies, and it is not going to help. Women should wear knee-length skirts (or longer) or business suits/slacks with matching blouses with a suit-style jacket. Neutral colored pantyhose, light make up at most, and professional hairstyles.

Neither gender should wear excessive jewelry. Avoid bright colors and distracting shirt or tie patterns. Remember: dress the part of a professional. If the position in which you are interviewing has no formal dress code, be certain to error on the side of conservative with a more professional look than not. If you feel you are over-dressed after arriving at your interview, you may take your jacket off and hang it on your chair.

Dressing for summer employment or a job where casual wear is appropriate.
In general, men should wear a long-sleeved button down shirt with Khakis and a belt. Women should wear nice pants and a blouse. Closed toed shoes are preferred.

Do not wear tank tops or spaghetti straps, and make sure the shirt you choose has proper coverage.

DURING THE INTERVIEW

During your interview, plan for two different types of questions: ***Real*** questions and ***What if*** questions.

***Real* questions** deal with specific events and accomplishments you have accumulated throughout your life. You will employ the **TopScore Top5** with your **Marketing Priorities** and **Core Values** interwoven within your answer.

What if questions deal with hypothetical situations. The oral board wants to judge your reaction and subsequent action to what are most likely uncomfortable situations. What if questions will include Situational, Leading, and Interpersonal questions. The interviewer or interview board will ask a wide range of questions with a specific objective. The board wants to get to know you to the best of their ability and to identify if you will fit their company.

Let's cover the real questions

Real Questions are questions you will answer using the *TopScore Top5* approach. Every answer will include:

Answer the question, and while answering the question, you will include the following in your answer:

1) Personal History (PH): 3-5 pieces
2) Personal Story (PS): 1 story
3) Company Knowledge (CK): 3-5 pieces
4) Keywords (KW): 3-5 pieces

The 3-5 pieces are a guideline and usually make for a professional sounding answer. You can have more than 5 but not less than 3.

TopScore Top5

Rule: Utilize the *TopScore Top5* to answer all Real questions.

Applying the TopScore Top5 will help you garner a top score or memorable answer in the interview. The actual answer to the interviewer's questions is only a small part of an excellent answer. The only reason the interviewer is asking the question is to engage you and to judge your eagerness, ability and suitability from the answer you provide. Important items you add to support your answers are what will get you hired. Remember, there are five parts to a great answer: Answer the question, add in some personal history, tell them a related personal story, show company knowledge and use keywords. Add each of these into your response, and you'll have a strong answer that will set you apart from the competition.

To truly grasp and implement the concepts discussed in this book, you will need to practice and practice, and when you have done that, practice some more! Practice with people who don't make you feel comfortable. This will help you to perform in the nerve-racking environment of an oral interview board or in front or an interviewer. Practice in front of the mirror, and in front of people, and while being recorded. The *TopScore* Practice Interview Scorecard facilitates this. Practicing your interview will ensure that you can incorporate the topics discussed in this book and identify weak areas of your interview in time for them to be corrected.

Understanding and implementing the *TopScore Top5* will guide you during your interview and set you apart from your competition. Your newfound confidence will give you momentum throughout the interview. *TopScore Top5* are the five things you need in every answer to a real question. Most interviews are about thirty minutes long during which time you will have between eight to ten *Real* questions. This time accounts for interviewees to elaborate on their answers by using the *TopScore Top5*. The people who simply provide basic answers will be finished with their interview in five minutes. For example, if there are eight questions, and you reply with five pieces of your personal history in every answer, the interviewer(s) will then know forty more things about you! This will make their decision to hire you a lot easier. Thirty minutes is not a lot of time to get to know somebody who you are going to spend the next 1 to 20 years with as a fellow employee. You would pick the ones that gave you the most information about themselves (*Personal History*), spoke your language (*Keywords*), who told you stories you will not forget (*Personal Story)* and who included why they would be a perfect fit based on their expert knowledge of you (*Company Knowledge*). Give the interviewer the information they want to hear.

To reiterate, the *TopScore Top5* approach applies only to the real questions about you and your answer should include:

1) Personal History (PH): 3-5 pieces
2) Personal Story (PS): 1 story
3) Company Knowledge (CK): 3-5 pieces
4) Keywords (KW): 3-5 pieces

#1. Answer the Question

Rule: Answer the question, the whole question. This might seem obvious, but part of the answer can often be missed. Some questions are multiple part questions in which interviewees fail to answer all parts of the question.

For example: Jane is 18 years old and applying for a job as a lifeguard at a local swim center.

Question: *What is the most important trait a Lifeguard must have and why do you feel it is so important?*

This is an example of a two-part question that needs two complete answers. Jane will also need to incorporate the *TopScore Top5* answer which includes Personal History (PH), Personal Stories (PS), Company Knowledge (CK) and Key Words (KW).

Answer: *I believe the most important trait a lifeguard needs is* (KW) *visual attention. As you know, visual scanning and attention by lifeguards can be described as observing, recording and making an assessment of the water area that is being surveyed. It is the very foundation of a successful lifeguard. I believe it is the trait or value, which, on a daily basis, saves countless swimmers from drowning. I know if you have* (KW) *visual attention as a lifeguard, you are (KW) committed,* (KW) *dependable,* (KW) *alert and aware and* (KW) *focused on the water.* (CK) *The times I have visited the Swim Center I have seen how your lifeguards* (KW) *exemplify this trait and are* (KW) *dedicated to their job, their entire crew, their community as well as the Swim Center. I was excited to see how* (KW) *professional the lifeguards are here (CK) at the Swim Center. I since learned about the various swim programs the swim center offers in which lifeguards need to watch over. Seniors water aerobics, (CK) scuba classes, and diving team training to name a few. I know that on any given weekend, the swim center has up to 400 people enjoying the pools a day. (CK) I know that when I* *see the* (KW) *dedication of your entire staff, that I would be proud to be a part of it. I believe my athletic background will be a great benefit to your company. I have played sports most of my life. I played (PH) soccer (PH) baseball (PH) basketball and was on the (PH) varsity swim team for 2 years in high school. (PS) I remember one swim meet that a few people were sick and I had to swim three events. I usually only swam one, but the coach had confidence that I could handle it. I did; I won all three of my events and we ended up (PH) state champions that year. Lifeguards are entrusted with people's most prized possessions every day, that being their safety as well as their families' safety. I look forward to the rewarding challenge of keeping the pool safe.*

We highly recommend that you restate a multiple-part question back to the board. This gives you the opportunity to let yourself hear what it is you need to cover. It also provides for good two-way communication. There is also no problem with asking the board to repeat the question to be sure you heard all parts of it. Here's an example:

Question: *Tell the board a time when you faced a challenge in life in which you learned a valuable lesson and how it affected you as a person.*

You would repeat: *"A time I faced a challenge in which I learned a valuable lesson and how I was affected was,"* and then continue with the *TopScore Top5 answer.*

It is perfectly acceptable to take five seconds to think about the question prior to answering. You will not be interrupted or scored down for taking the time to think before you speak.

The TopScore Top5 will greatly aid you because it provides structure to your response and will prevent rambling. When you have hit all five parts of your answer, you are done! The hardest part is learning how to segue from one part of your answer to the other to make it sound natural and fluid. The TopScore Top5 do not necessarily need to be addressed in any particular order, but each of these aspects must be addressed to receive a top score for your answer.

#2. Personal History

Rule: Get your fishing lines in the water.

This is your Personal History that consists of particular things the oral board will want to hear. For example, such things as where you were born, where you grew up, schools you attended, degrees you earned, your family, certifications and achievements as well as your hobbies, sports, trades and job history. Think of each piece of your personal history as tags and titles you have accomplished throughout your life: student, son/daughter, waiter, soccer player, volunteer, etc. The more fishing lines you put in the water, the better your chances of hooking something. Hooking something is equivalent to getting an interviewer to associate with you. This is the first step in building any relationship. If you talk about things they can relate to, they will naturally form a bond and view you as a likely candidate to hire. The closest people in your life will have thousands of these lines connected with you, thus you have a close relationship with each other.

Your "personal life" personal history will vary with the nature of the job and the life experiences you have had. For promotional interviews as well as professional- type jobs, your personal history from living life may not be as critical as your personal history from your job life. Past performances in the field for which you are interviewing will take precedence over conveying where you worked in high school or how you walked the Camino de Santiago trail after graduating from college.

This is a real-life example of how your life experiences can help you relate to your interviewer. My friend Jeff and I went to an interview with the same company. Upon entering the interview, I thought I had it in the bag. I just knew I was going to score higher than Jeff. After the interview, I expressed to Jeff how well I felt I had done. Jeff expressed that his interview had gone a bit differently than mine. Jeff's interview was going as expected when it came up that he had a 1965 Mustang that he just finished restoring, and as chance would have it, one of the interviewers across the table had the exact same Mustang. They spent the rest of the interview talking about their cars, where to get parts for their cars and trading technical tips. Jeff just happened to have just the right "fishing line" to catch one of the interviewers and he did so, hook, line, and sinker. And guess who got the job? That's right, Jeff! Do you have to have such a "fishing line" to get a job? Of course not, and what's more, it rarely happens; however, you never know what the interviewer or the members of the interview board will relate to. Simply stated, if they can relate to you, it is much easier for them to picture you as the ideal employee they desire to have as part of their team. It is easier to work with people who share common interests with you. Get those fishing lines in the water!

Homework

Write down your top 30 or more things you want the interviewer to know about you, your Personal History (PH). Remember, the more they know about you, the better. Use a separate piece of paper, or write your notes in your Interview Rule Book Workbook.

#3. Personal Story (PS)

Rule: Employ stories they will remember.

Think of your Personal History (PH) as the words, and your Personal Story (PS) as the actions.

You need to stand out to the oral interview board or interviewer, having a solid Personal Story is imperative. The Personal Story you choose to tell should support what you shared in your Personal History. Anyone can boast about his or her excellent leadership qualities, but few can demonstrate these qualities. Talk is cheap and actions speak louder than words. It needs to be clear to the oral board or interviewer that you are providing a personal story that actually happened, and that the story supports what you described within your personal history. If you talk about being a good leader, you should have a good Personal Story to support it. It will usually start with something like "*One time I...*" or "*I remember when I...*". This is where you will employ your Marketing Strategies interlaced with Core Competencies. We will cover these later in the book, and they will help you narrow down some of your valuable stories.

Here is an example of someone interviewing for a Verizon Wireless Store sales position demonstrating the use of a Personal Story.

Question: "*Explain what you consider is a personal weakness of yours.*"

Answer: "*Public speaking is an area in which I am working to improve. Sitting here in front of you reminds me of the* *feeling I had before a speech I performed in the fifth grade.* (PS) *I was running for* (PH) *student body vice president, and when I stood in front of my entire grade school to give my speech, I completely froze. The kids started to giggle and I stepped away from the podium to gather myself before I tried again. This happened about three times before the principal finally leaned in behind me and whispered, "Why don't you start with your name?" With that suggestion, my well-rehearsed speech came back to me. I stepped up to the microphone and* (KW) *delivered.* (PH) *As it turned out, I won the election. I guess it's mostly about being memorable when you're in elementary school.*

Since that event, I've gotten much more comfortable speaking in front of people, but, in that moment while I was figuring out public speaking in elementary school, at the back of the auditorium stood both my parents supporting me, just as they had while I practiced the speech over and over. I do not consider my public speaking a strength, but I can assure you that it is much better than it used to be.

I know here, at Verizon, that talking with customers is a major part of the job as well as teaching (CK). *I know that Verizon not only sells phones and mobile equipment (CK) but also offers numerous classes to customers who make mobile purchases. (CK) Talking about how great Verizon products are and teaching customers about their purchases is something that I am looking forward to. I mentioned that my* (PH) *parents encouraged me back in fifth grade. They continue to do so as they did on the phone this morning prior to this interview. "*

#4. Company Knowledge (CK)

Rule: Look on the internet for useful information about the company and the position for which you are interviewing.

Company knowledge and knowledge about the position showcases your interest in the company .and accomplishes two things. First, it demonstrates your interest in and commitment to your future employer. It proves that you've embraced the challenge, that you take your future job seriously, and shows sincerity and a commitment to be a part of their company. Second, it will help to ensure that you've selected the company and position that is best suited for you. When possible, incorporate the company's future plans and include the company's mission statement and value statement in your answers. For example: *"I believe in AFLAC's mission statement. It states... therefore, I would..."* In addition, learn basic facts about the company in which you are applying such as who started the company and why and basic facts and figures about the company in which you are applying. This will give you one more edge over the competition.

General history of your work field is also important to master. You need to become a student of all aspects of your profession. Who is responsible for the greatest advances in your field? Learn basic facts and figures involving those in your field. You never know when that type of information may become a valuable edge that you will have against others applying for the same position.

Another way to learn the specifics about a company is to schedule a job shadow. A job shadow is when you follow someone around who is currently in the position you wish to have. It allows you to see exactly what a person in that position does as well as gives you plenty of opportunities to ask questions. Job shadows are also extremely important for gaining information regarding the company to which you are applying. If at all possible, schedule a job shadow. If the company you are applying to does not allow job shadows, you will have to do more online research. Become a Twitter follower and a friend on Facebook. This will give you the latest news the company.

You can also try to talk to some of the employees who are in the same position you are applying for. Obviously, every job will be different so you will have to adapt it to your specific field or position for which you are applying. As far as the job shadow, you will have to adapt that as well. Years ago I had a friend who was applying for a job at the county 911 dispatch center. I told her to go down and do a job shadow. She was able to schedule an eight-hour day where she could sit in dispatch and see exactly what they do. While she was there, she learned a lot about what really goes on behind the scenes every day. When she was at her interview, she mentioned something about how calls were dispatched, and the interviewers asked how she knew this "inside information." She told them that she had spent eight hours sitting in on calls and asking questions. The interviewers were amazed that she had put forth so much effort. They told her that they have never seen such determination before. She got the job.

It will not always be possible to sit next to a person in the job you are applying for, but see if there is a way. Maybe you could just meet with someone who currently does the job. This would give you a chance to discover "inside" information that cannot be found on the internet. Maybe you will hear about things that are that are not going smooth or problems you will be faced with. This will give you time to come up with possible solutions. This could also give you more insight to determine if you are a good fit for this company and if you would be happy in that position.

Basic Rules for Job Shadowing

Rule: When you show up, be part of the team.

Rule: Do The Job Shadow! A company job shadow is the perfect opportunity to learn about the company and meet your future co-workers.

Rule: Wear appropriate clothing.

Rule: Leave your phone in the car. If you want to take some notes, use a pen and paper.

Rule: If appropriate, bring a gift. Bring in some cookies or something to show you appreciate the time they are spending with you.

Rule: Speak less and listen more. Many people engaged in their first job shadow get quite excited. This leads to the motor mouth syndrome. It should go without saying that profanity and other unprofessional speech has no place in this environment. Remember, the job shadow serves as a layer of unofficial screening for the company.

Rule: Bring your own meals. Plan on providing your own meals if you are shadowing during lunch or dinner.

Rule: Follow Instructions.

Rule: Jump in and help! If there is something you can help with, jump in if you are allowed.

Rule: Have your job shadow questions ready. Have a list of questions that you would like to know about the company. These are things that you will use as Company Knowledge in the interview and are things that were not readily found through a cursory online search.

Rule: Confidentiality. Be mindful of what you see and share.

Rule: Best Behavior. Remember, the entire time you are on your job shadow, you are going through an unofficial interview with members of the company. Greet everyone you can with a friendly smile and firm handshake.

Rule: Ask questions.

The following are sample questions you can address during your job shadow if you were not able to find the answer through the company's website or online search. Remember that if you are asking questions in which answers are easily found on the internet, you are not showcasing your initiative.

Who is the company CEO, and what is their history in the company?

How many employees are in the company? ?

What is the company structure?

What cities, states and countries is the company in?

When was the company started? By whom?

What is the salary for each level and what benefits are offered?

What type of retirement is offered?

What is the work schedule? Overtime? Is overtime mandatory?

How many jobs are available?

What is the company history?

Why and how is this company different from its competitors?

What are the company's goals? How can you help achieve them?

What does the future hold for this company?

What does an average day consist of?

For which nonprofit groups or fundraisers does the company raise money?

Homework

Write down 20 significant facts regarding the company and the specific position you are applying for. These will be found online and during your job shadow. Use a separate piece of paper, or write your notes in your Interview Rule Book Workbook.

#5. Keywords (KW)

Rule: Use Keywords, especially words popular with the company in which you are interviewing. Profession, trade, or business terminology can also be a great tool for you to talk the talk.

You should utilize these important *Keywords* to highlight your experience and accomplishments. These keywords are so important, you shouldn't be surprised to see the oral board or interviewer make notes each time you use one in your answers.

For example: you are asked a simple question such *as "What is your favorite color?"* If you simply answer *"Blue"*, you will not get hired. You need to give the interviewer or board enough information to understand why you chose blue. Instead, give an answer like the following:

My favorite color is blue. Blue has been my favorite color for as long as I can remember. My first (PH) *hockey jersey was a blue Hartford Whalers jersey. Playing with the Whalers was how I learned the value of the* (KW) *teamwork and* (KW) *camaraderie associated with being part of a winning team. My friends and I were not the best players in the league, but we played as a team. We worked together towards the same goal, and we managed to win the* (PH) *championship in 2008.* (PS) *I can still remember the great feeling of skating around and passing the trophy from teammate to teammate, plus the fun we had at the celebration afterward. I have played team sports my entire life. I grew up playing* (PH) *soccer and then transitioned to* (PH) *football and eventually* (PH) *ice hockey. (CK) I know AFLAC, which has the color blue in its logo is one big team that gains from the* (KW) *strength of all involved. Working as a* (KW) *team will only make one stronger and faster and is more enjoyable than working alone. I know from doing research on AFLAC that AFLAC provides protection for over (CK) 50 million people worldwide. This highest level of service can only be provided by its (CK) 95,000 agents worldwide working as one smooth operating team.*

Despite the simplicity of the question about your favorite color, good use of *Key Words* (KW) along with the rest of the *TopScore Top5* will tell the oral board exactly what they need to know about you. The sample answer above told the board several things. The board now knows that you play hockey, you work well in a team environment, you enjoy the camaraderie of working together and that you are able to obtain goals through synergy. The board learned all of this by simply listening to you explain why your favorite color is blue.

Remember: *Keywords* are simply additional segues to an opportunity to tell the board more about you. Each keyword must have substance behind it. The last thing the board wants to hear when they ask "What is your favorite color?" is a canned answer. You need to always involve all aspects of the TopScore Top5 into your answer. Remember: the keywords are the words that are important to the specific job, trade, profession or company to which you are applying.

Examples of Real Questions:
Rule: Answer Real questions using the *TopScore* Top5 approach.

Real questions will probably be asked first. Odds are, you will be asked a question similar to *"Tell us about yourself."* This is a *Real* question as well as an icebreaker. Below are examples of *Real* questions and possible answers. Remember, the suggestions provided should give you a good idea of where to start your answer and are not your answers. Remember: All aspects of the TopScore Top5 must be incorporated in your response.

Question: *What impact does stress and pressure have on a person's decision-making skills?*

Answer: *Stress and pressure will stimulate a person in one of two ways: negatively or positively. Negative stimulation* *will result in a poor decision or can lead to quick decisions, both resulting in mistakes or compromising* (KW) *safety. As a high school student in California, I played team sports. They included* (PH) *soccer,* (PH) *hockey,* (PH) *track and* (PH) *swimming. I learned a great deal about* (KW) *teamwork,* (KW) *camaraderie and* (KW) *leadership. One night, I also learned about peer pressure.* (PS) *One time, one of my friends from the varsity soccer team talked me into sneaking out for the night to toilet paper another teammate's home. I knew if I was caught, I would have to answer to my disappointed parents as well as my friend's parents, but, at the same time, I didn't want to be a considered a wimp. I wanted to be considered one of "the gang", so I gave in. Sure enough, my dad caught me. I then had to approach my friend's parents and confess to the toilet paper job.*

(PS) *A positive reaction can make certain people more efficient. When people are trained to operate during times of high stress and are equipped with the proper tools for the job, their* (KW) *situational awareness is high.* (CK) *Here at XROK, the training department is recognized as one of the best in the field.* (CK) *XROK recognizes and makes training a high priority within the company. More importantly, you train your members to learn how to deal with and work in stressful situations.*

(PS) *Last summer, while dining at a local restaurant, a gentleman who was sitting a few tables away from me suffered a major heart attack. A person nearby witnessed the event, rushed over to the unconscious man and started a quick assessment. He then told another nearby customer to call 9-1-1. Little did I know, the* (PH) *CPR training I completed five years earlier during my senior year of high school was about to be put to the test. I sprang from my chair without hesitation and assisted the bystander with moving the patient to the floor. The bystander asked me if I knew C.P.R. and I responded, "Yes, I do." He told me to perform chest compressions. I kneeled beside the patient, and without even thinking, I located the notch where the lower part of the rib meets the center of the chest and began counting as I compressed the patient's chest. I continued compressions for five minutes until the fire department arrived on the scene. This obviously went from a calm night having dinner to a very significant and stressful event. That evening, I learned a lot about how I would respond in a stressful situation. I had previous training, albeit five years prior, and despite the passage of time, I had perfect memory recall and was able to stay focused and calm while performing CPR.*

Let's examine the response above to see what aspects of the TopScore Top5 were addressed:

Answer the Question: The question was answered and a positive spin was put on it.

Personal History: High school athlete, varsity soccer, hockey, track and swimming, family.

Personal Story: Peer pressure story and story of performing CPR to man in restaurant.

Keywords: *Team, teamwork, camaraderie and leadership.*

Company Knowledge: Talking about the training department being recognized as one of the best in the field demonstrates you have studied this specific company.

Here's another example:

Question: *We know what you can offer XROK, but what can the XROK offer you?*

Answer: *Working for this company can offer me* (KW) *security,* (KW) *camaraderie and a true sense of* (KW) *accomplishment. Your* (CK) *training department is well respected amongst other companies. This company also has the best* (CK) *sales-to-member ratio in the industry and* (KW) *progressive training that includes (CK) web design and (CK) CPS sheets.* (PS) *During my senior year of high school, I was honored to be the* (PH) *captain of the* (PH) *football team as well as the* (PH) *baseball team.* (PS) *I can still remember the honor I felt when my coach said he chose me to be captain because, day in and day out, I always brought my best to the team. The single, most important lesson my coaches provided me for my success was to set clear expectations. Clear expectations as a captain of the team included but were not limited to my general conduct, my* (KW) *positive attitude, my* (KW) *work ethic and the level of skill I was to deliver on the field. The expectations they placed on me were all I needed to bring my very best day-in and day-out. If I did not mention this before, I am extremely competitive.* (PS) *It is my competitive nature to exceed any standard set before me.* (CK) *I have read your company's Standards, Mission Statement and Vision Statement. I clearly understand what this company expects of me.*

Let's examine the response above to see what aspects of the TopScore Top5 were addressed.

Answer the Question: Again, the question was answered. *The company offers me security and safety with the best available training. They offer an opportunity to be a part of their team. XROK provides clear expectations from the guiding documents such as Mission and Vision statements.*

Personal History: California, High school, football and baseball. Captain of both teams

Personal Story: Promoted to captain. Competitive Nature to exceed standards.

Keywords: Respected, progressive, safe, camaraderie, positive attitude, and work ethic.

Company Knowledge: Knows company members receive web design and CPS report training. Showed knowledge of the Standards and the Mission Statement.

Here is another example:

Question: *What do you believe is the most important trait for a person to have?*

Answer: *I am* (PH) *twenty-nine years old with a* (PH) *wife and* (PH) *two young kids. I grew up playing team sports like* (PH) *football and* (PH) *hockey. I am now in the* (PH) *construction and remodeling business and often find myself with keys and codes to people's homes. I do not take this responsibility lightly. The success of my business rides not only on customer satisfaction (KW) once the project is complete, but also how I treated them and their homes. A customer may be happy with the outcome of the project, but if they do not trust me or like me as a person, they will never refer me to a friend. My business depends on those referrals. I can tell you this: there is nothing in anyone's home that is worth the price of my (KW) integrity. More than anything, stealing and dishonesty are not in my genetic make-up.*

(PS) *Just the other day, I was at one of the local box stores returning a few small items that I did not use on my last remodel. When I handed the cashier the items to scan and return, she told me that they were not on my receipt. I then handed her the debit card I used to purchase the items, and again, she said the items were not purchased on that card. Without proof, the cashier could not give me cash, but would have to give me in-store credit instead. She began to set up a gift card for the balance and then it dawned on me: I had the correct receipt and the correct card. I double checked the receipt and realized that I was never charged. I had purchased several items at the same time, and somehow, four items were never scanned. I explained that I had purchased four identical items and had used two, but wanted to return the other two. She asked me what I wanted to do. I declined the gift card, and asked to be charged for the two items I used but did not pay for.*

I live with (KW) integrity every day of my life, and I understand the importance it plays in life, business and especially with your company. I know I can be counted on to continue the (CK) *tradition of* (KW) *honesty,* (KW) *integrity and* (KW) *trustworthiness of this company.*

Let's examine the response above to see what aspects of the TopScore Top5 were addressed.

Answer the Question: The candidate answered the question with *integrity* being his answer and that nothing in anyone's home was worth the price of his/her integrity.

Personal History: Twenty-nine years old, wife, two young kids, football, hockey, construction and remodeling business.

Personal Story: Not paying for all his items at a local box store and discovering it after the fact and paying for them when it figured it out.

Keywords: Satisfaction, integrity, value, and honesty trustworthiness.

Company Knowledge: Knows the long-standing traditions of the company and can be counted on to uphold them.

Let's look at another example:

Question: *Describe a time when you were faced with change. How did you react?*

Answer: *Change equals stress. Some people allow stress to control their actions, and others have a way of embracing change and subsequently the stress that goes with it. I've learned to embrace stress as a* (KW) *motivator to accomplish the tasks I have in front of me. Some people might let stress control their lives and slow down or halt their progress. If you look at it as a threat or problem instead of an opportunity, stress will control you. When I graduated from* (PH) *college with a* (PH) *4.0 GPA and an (PH) A.S. degree in science, a part of me didn't want to leave the area I lived in because of the* (KW) *family,* (KW) *camaraderie and service I experienced as part of my* (PH) *fraternity. Even though my life was about to experience a big change, I knew it was time for me move on and put my life experiences to work. Once I moved, I was able to make many new friends at my new school as well as a* (PH) *volunteer for the local Boys and Girls Club. I know family and* (KW) *service is important in your company, (CK) so much so that it is one of the three words of your company motto. In college , we were required to do a minimal amount of community service.* (PS) *I consistently exceeded that number of hours and posted the highest number of service hours for two consecutive semesters. I mentioned earlier* *that some look at stress as a problem while others look at it as an opportunity. During 2013, your company had the (CK) highest returns since 2008 and also gained an additional (CK) 5% of the market share. I look forward to helping this company continue to grow.*

Let's examine the response above to see what aspects of the TopScore Top5 were addressed.

Answer the Question: This was a two-part question and both parts were addressed. The change was that the candidate moved away from everything he/she had known. He/she moved far away from family and friends and embraced the change because it provided motivation to immediately make new friends at a new school as well as being a part of the community as a volunteer.

Personal History: The interview board now knows this interviewee graduated from college with a 4.0 GPA and an A.S. degree, was a member of a fraternity and enjoys building relationships.

Personal Story: The interviewer(s) knows you excel at public service through community service projects.

Key Words: Family, camaraderie, motivation and service were all addressed.

Company knowledge: The board knows you value the same things they do as represented on their department shield. You also mentioned the company's growth.

Now Check Out Two More Answers.

The key to making this type of interview technique work for you is to practice and practice and then, when you think you're ready, practice some more, so, to help you with your practice, here's two more answers with answers based on the TopScore Top5, both answering the following question: *"Tell me about a challenge that you overcame."*

We will answer it from the position of two different interviewees seeking two totally different job opportunities. Pay particular attention to how each interviewee uses the TopScore Top5 system to answer the same question. The first will be a 16-year-old male named Luke. He is interviewing for his first job at a local landscaping company where he is interviewing for a lawn mowing position. The second will be a 28-year-old female named Ginny. She is interviewing as a Web developer for an up and coming tech company.

The first answer is with 16-year-old Luke:

Once again, the **question**. *Tell us about a challenge you had to overcome?*

Answer: *In my short sixteen years of life, I have had to overcome many challenges. As a (PH) son, as a (PH) big brother with two little sisters, as a (PH)(KW) competitive skateboarder since I was nine, as a (PH) grandson to my grandfather who lost his battle with cancer six months ago, and I have also had challenges as a student. (PS) Last year, I had a (PH)"C" on my report card at the halfway point of the semester. That was a very challenging time of hard work and complete (KW) dedication on my part to bring the grade up. For some reason, (PH) math was extremely hard to learn during my 8th grade year. I (PH) signed myself up to be tutored three times a week, and I also (PH) sacrificed my lunchtime from time to time to work with my math teacher. The hard work ended up paying off as I was able to bring my grade up to an "A".*

I mentioned my grandfather who passed away not long ago. (PS) Last summer, due to his treatments, he was unable to mow his lawn, so I took care of it. His lawnmower was at least 30 years old. During the summer heat in July, while mowing his lawn, a wheel broke off the axle. At first, I thought it was a perfect excuse to quit during that 102-degree day. But the reality of it was that I wanted to finish it so my grandfather wouldn't have to worry about it, plus quitting is not in my nature. I went over to his wood scraps in his wood shop and cut a round piece the same size of the broken wheel. I drilled a hole in it, put it on the axle, fastened it with a bolt and was able to finish the job. So if you have any lawn mowers here that might need a wooden wheel, I can fix them for you (said with a smile).

Luke continued: *One of the reasons I applied with your landscape company is because (CK)you have a (KW)great reputation of doing (KW)high quality work. I know (CK) you have been in business since 1990. I read one review online from a customer, which stated, (CK)"they mow my lawn as if it was theirs." That's the kind of landscaper I would be for you if I were hired.*

Now, let's break Luke's answer down.

Because Luke prepared himself with *Interview Rule Book* he was able to use what was available for this answer from the TopScore Top5 and nailed it.

Answer the question: Luke answered the question, but more importantly he took advantage of the opportunity to get lots of extra good information to the interviewer.

Personal History: Luke spoke of the different tags he has worn that have had challenges. A son, a big brother of two little sisters, a grandson, a student, and a competitive skateboarder.

Personal Story: Luke was able to provide two good stories from his short life that helps support his candidacy for the position. His math lesson, where he showed his hard work, dedication, and perseverance. The better of the two stories included Luke mowing lawns. He took the interviewer out of the room and to his grandfather's yard on a hot summer day. He hit on the challenge he had to overcome, and the end result of using some innovation and self-reliance to work through a problem in order to complete the job. He just made it as easy as possible to the board or interviewer in their prediction of what he might be like if they end up hiring him. They would conclude that Luke works hard, takes pride in his work and can work through problems on his own. For the company, Luke is going to be an easy decision as he has provided them with a story that they can easily predict how he would perform if was hired.

Company Knowledge: Luke mentioned a review that he read an online review and knew the year the business was started. This shows the interviewers that he had done his research and was not just throwing his name into the hat for any landscaping company.

Keywords: He communicated that he was dedicated, a hard worker that was committed and one that did not quit.

Bottom Line: Luke was able to get all he could out of this single question. He was prepared and used the TopScore Top5 as is supposed to be utilized.

Let's look at one more example. Ginny is a 28-year-old female interviewing with a startup tech company for a web developer position. Web developers create everything you see on the web, from the special effects to the search functionality.

Once again, **the question**: *Tell us about a challenge you had to overcome?*

Ginny quickly reflects in her mind the job description for the position for which she was interviewing. This lets her take full advantage of valuable real estate in which she can provide great content with her answer. Ginny read the following job posting for the web developer position:

Our web developers at Z Innovation work closely with our project managers, strategists and design team members to develop specifications and make recommendations on the use of new and emerging technologies. Programming, graphic design and database administration are all elements of this position.

Z Innovations: Everything we do is defined by the mantra THINK, CREATE, LAUNCH

Responsibilities:

> *Work closely with Project Managers and other members of the Development Team to both develop detailed, specification documents and establish timely completion of deliverables.*
>
> *Engage in outside-the-box thinking to provide high value-of-service to clients.*
>
> *Alert colleagues to emerging technologies or applications and the opportunities.*

Required Skills

Self-starter with strong self-management skills

Ability to organize and manage multiple priorities

Upon thinking about the job position and this job description, Ginny gave the following **answer** to the question:

I have had numerous (KW) challenges, or in my (KW) positive outlook "opportunities to experience life" as a (PH) daughter of a military father, (PH) a single mother of two incredible kids who have selective hearing, (PH) a runner who has completed eleven marathons, (PH) a student and, yes, as (PH)an employee web developer. Let me share with you challenges and some very incredible (KW) learning opportunities I experienced at ABC TECH.

(PS)I was originally brought on as an intern for a six-month period. Those six months turned into seven years of full time employment. While I was interning, the company was growing faster than expected. Usually, tech interns are assisting with phone calls, fetching coffee and setting up meeting locations and times. Basically, they do support work to help the web developers out. As a very (KW) organized person, I assisted with taking notes for a couple of the web developers during their meetings, and during one particular meeting with a client, there was a project that was very similar to my final project I completed in college. My web developer, Ben, gave a quote of 50 Hours with a completion date of 45 days. The client insisted that it be done in 25 days. I had a sidebar conversation with Ben. I assured him that I could get it done and have it to him in three weeks. Bob said, "Have it in two weeks in case I need to fix it." I accepted the challenge, but knew I would

have to successfully manage multiple priorities. With hard work, (KW) sacrifice and minimal sleep, I was able to have it on Ben's desk within 14 days. Ben was very happy with the end product. I would like to tell you that it was easy, but it wasn't. Not the complexity of the task but trying to get it completed on my own time at home while running kids to soccer, making dinner, doing laundry, helping with their homework as well as all the other odd jobs we do as parents. Coming up with an extra 50 hours of free time and still getting the rest of things covered was a challenge. It was truly self-management and managing multiple priorities. I truly felt like I was one of the "real" web developers. Everything I had worked so hard in school on for so long was alive with emotion in me on this project. I did not have work software to use, only my home computer, so I (KW) thought a little outside the box. I was able to use the new and emerging software technologies loaded on my PC eight months earlier when I was still a student in college. Ben said he appreciated the out of the box thinking and praised me for being a self-starter and able to get the task complete without calling on him for help. Without a high level of my self-discipline and organization skills, this task would not have been possible. If I were hired, I would bring the same level of effort, skills, and ability to overcome future challenges/opportunities to Z Innovations. A timely completion of deliverables is important to Z Innovations. For Z Innovation, this means that I am committed to delivering great work by the deadline.

I find this job opportunity very exciting for numerous reasons. (PH)(CK) I have worked for a start-up and helped grow it into a successful business over the past seven years. I know my experience, work ethic, ability to be a self-starter and, more importantly, my ability to work as a (CK) team player would be a great fit here at Z Innovations. I embrace and welcome your company's mantra, (CK) THINK, CREATE, LAUNCH.

Let's break down Ginny's answer while utilizing the TopScore Top5.

Because Ginny also prepared herself with *Interview Rule Book,* she was able to use the TopScore Top5 system and nail the answer.

Answer the question: Ginny answered the question, but more importantly, she took advantage of the opportunity to get lots of extra, good information to the interviewer. She thoroughly answered the question.

Personal History (PH): Ginny spoke of the different tags she has worn in life that have come with various challenges. She mentioned being daughter of a military father, being a single mother, a marathon runner, a student, and a "SUCCESSFUL" web developer. (Note the word "successful" she added. They are looking to hire a successful person, and she just claimed that title. A great use of a keyword at a great time.)

Personal Story (PS): Ginny shared the story of taking on an assignment and successfully completing it. More importantly, her story showcased her in the same light in which she is trying to get hired. Furthermore, Ginny stated, *I truly felt like I was one of the web developers.* She also hit on the challenge she had to overcome and made it as easy as possible for the board or interviewer to draw an only conclusion: that she would do the same for Z Innovations if hired.

Company Knowledge (CK): Knowing this is a startup company, she shares her success with a previous start up. She mentions her success in working as part of a team. This was highlighted under the responsibilities for the job. She mentions the company's mantra THINK, CREATE, LAUNCH.

Keywords (KW): She includes outside the box thinking. She also talks about her high level of organizational skills, which is a required skill from the job description. She speaks of completing work in a timely manner.

Bottom Line: Ginny was able to get all she could out of this single question. She was prepared and used the TopScore Top5 as is supposed to be utilized.

Question Type #2: The "*What If*" Questions

These are the second set of questions. These questions can be posed as statements followed by a question and usually follow the real questions.

Rule: Remember, these questions form make-believe scenarios.

Rule: Steer the oral board members or interviewer in the direction you want them to go.

Take the board members or interviewer to the make-believe world. Do *not* add Personal Stories or Personal History. Some Keywords and Company Knowledge may be appropriate but are not required like they are in the ***Real*** questions. Don't rush through these questions, even if you have heard the question before and already know exactly what you are going to say. Slow down and act as though you have never heard it before. Rushing through a question might cause you to leave out information that could separate you from the other candidates.

What If questions include:

1) Leading Questions
2) Situational Questions
3) Interpersonal Questions

LEADING QUESTION

A leading question is a question that will attempt to lead you into assuming something negative.

Example: While working in an office job for a local medical center, you see a fellow employee loading his or her personal bag with a large quantity of samples that are meant to be given out to patients. What are you going to do?

Rule: Don't assume there is a problem. Only assume positive. By assuming negative, you may be viewed as being angry or overly negative all of the time. By assuming the positive, you assume that the other coworkers you work with are professional, trustworthy and acting in the best interest of the company, just as you are.

You could start your answer by saying: *People who work for this company are known for being honest and trustworthy. After all, they are entrusted with people's personal health information. I would assume that the person was not doing anything wrong. Maybe they were told to load them up and take them to another office or doctor.*

Rule: Defuse the bomb

Leading questions are purposely attempting to lead you into assuming something negative. This is crucial for you to understand: leading questions are designed to make you believe that something negative is occurring, and if you do, you will fail the question. When an interviewer or the oral board asks you a leading question, it's akin to them lighting the fuse to a bomb. If you know how to diffuse it or direct it in a better direction, you will be successful. There are a wide range of topics they can ask you about including theft, drinking and drug use.

Example #1

Question: You see your supervisor drinking from a flask and know that drinking alcohol on the job is against company policy. What are you going to do?

At this point, the fuse is lit. It is time for you to attempt to defuse the bomb.

Response: *Yeah, we bought that for him for his birthday; it's our running joke, he keeps water in it.*

Now, the bomb is diffused. The interviewer(s) will not let you get away that easy, but they now know you understand the game. The interviewer may then add, *"You smell alcohol on his breath."*

You should continue to assume the positive.

Response: *This is a job of professionals. There are other things that could cause his breath to smell of alcohol like cold medicine or mouthwash. I don't think there is a problem.*

Soon, the interviewer or interviewing board will then give you enough information to show you that something *is* wrong. In this situation, the person in question is undoubtedly drinking on the job. Once there is no doubt, it is then your responsibility to correct the problem, taking it up the chain of command beginning at the lowest level and continue until an acceptable outcome is obtained.

Example #2

Question: "*You see a coworker taking money out of the cash jar in the break room refrigerator, what do you do?"*

Don't initially assume the worst possible situation and make certain you take the time to craft an appropriate answer to the question.

An example approach could be that your fellow worker probably put a larger bill in the cash jar and was now just making change for it. The interview board might continue the question by adding to the circumstances of the event. Stay positive and only positive until they provide enough information to prove that the worker was actually stealing. By staying with positive responses, you can control the direction of your answers. If they provide enough information to prove guilt and if what the employee in question was doing is illegal or against company policy, then you must make sure the issue is addressed and is prosecuted to the fullest extent of the law. You owe it to your employer and to your profession to do so. Remember: this is a job of professionals and there is no room for illegal behavior.

Response: *This is a job of professionals; we need to uphold our co-workers and employers' trust. I should be able to trust him to get change from a jar in the soda refrigerator or there is no room for him in this company.*

Notice in the response above that only a positive outcome was assumed. As mentioned earlier, the interviewer or interview board might pursue the situation and add to the circumstances of the situation.

Interviewer or Interview Board: *"There has been a lot of money missing."*

Response: *I would make a note of it in my head, but I don't have any proof there is an actual problem. I would trust that the worker is doing the right thing until I have PROOF to the contrary.*

You still have the opportunity to assume positive. Because you trust your fellow workers, you can trust they will pay it back. At some point in time, the board might state there is actual theft happening. At this point, you too must acknowledge the illegal behavior. You must address the problem and do whatever it takes to rectify the situation using the Chain of Command. The Chain of Command process provides the opportunity to deal with any situation at the lowest level possible. Be prepared to explain how you will address and correct the problem. This piece of the question could be just as important as addressing the leading aspect of the question. When formulating your answer "treat others as you want to be treated" would apply. You should start by privately and respectfully addressing the issue with the worker in question. Wouldn't you expect the same respect from them? Perhaps you'll discover a personal issue provoking this behavior. Obviously, regardless of the personal problem, it's still not acceptable, but it shows compassion and respect, and it presents an opportunity for them to rectify the situation before it escalates. This would be an uncomfortable situation, but inform the worker in question that he needs to speak with the supervisor, and you can offer to go with him or her. If the supervisor does not address the situation, take it up the chain to the next highest rank. If the issue is still not resolved, keep going up the chain. You know this is not acceptable behavior, and it needs to be stopped. Remember, this is more than just a petty theft from a soda jar at work. Each employee is an ambassador of the company and is trusted.

Situational Interview Question

Situational questions ask how you might handle future issues or opportunities. They may be stated like: "*What would you do if…*" Your interview board is simply seeing how you go about using your experience, intelligence, and knowledge to solve problems they present to you. These, more than likely, will be problems that the position you are applying for has to deal with. The more reason for you to do a job shadow, if possible, or interview those holding the position you are interviewing for. This is one we really can't help you on except to tell you about it ahead of time, and to tell you to **do your homework**!

Interpersonal Interview Questions

Interpersonal Skills are the skills we use every day while dealing with people. *Interpersonal skills* are also known as social skills, people skills or emotional intelligence. People who have great interpersonal skills are naturally easy to get along with and can usually relate to those going through stressful situations. Obviously, strong interpersonal skills are a necessity for work. It is important to maintain and grow these skills to build trust and integrity. People with good interpersonal skills will generally thrive in a team atmosphere. They possess effective communication skills with other employees and external customers.

I recently attended a friend's 50th anniversary party. After the party ended, I offered to assist with cleaning up the plates and cups as well as vacuuming the floors and putting away the tables and chairs. I volunteered under the direction of an 80-year-old gentleman who was the type of person who wanted things done his way. He had a particular process for clearing tables and putting the table and chairs away. Though it was clear there was a faster way, out of respect and patience, I followed his lead. Sure, it may have taken ten minutes longer than how I would have done it, but I was aware that he needed followers more than I needed to fulfill my natural desire to lead. This would be an example of an interpersonal skill.

You are with the same people for 40 hours a week. There will be times when your co-workers will get on your nerves. If your children (whom you care so much about) can get under your skin, imagine how someone whom you have no physical relations can set you off! Interpersonal skills are things that you display on a daily basis, not just when at your job.

If you feel your Interpersonal Skills are lacking, TopScore recommends researching and reading books based on emotional intelligence. These books include emotional intelligence tests showing your strengths and weaknesses within your own interpersonal skills.

Think about where and when you have displayed positive interpersonal skills and write a list of five times you have displayed unique interpersonal skills. Trust us; you have them, even if you are a high school graduate who is just beginning to enter the workforce.

Interpersonal Questions

Interpersonal questions are designed to explore how you and your fellow employees relate to one another on a daily basis including possible conflicts you may have.

Rule: Try to solve conflicts at the lowest level possible. If it does not get solved, then move up the chain of command to your next supervisor.

Rule: Get all the information before addressing the problem. Gather your facts, not rumors.

Your responses to interpersonal questions allow the interviewer or interview board the opportunity to judge your ability to deal with conflict and to obtain a viable solution for the parties involved at the lowest supervisory level possible. Being able to get along and resolve conflicts at the lowest level possible is paramount to operating as a successful team in any business or profession. It is important for the interviewer or interview board to know you are capable of resolving conflicts professionally.

Let's look at an example:

Question: *"You have noticed that a fellow employee has not been completing his job assignments, leaving more work for you on a continuing basis. This is frustrating since his apparent lazy attitude is adding significantly to your workload. How would you handle this situation?"*

To address interpersonal conflicts, start at the source. In the example above, you should speak directly to the employee in question, express your concerns, and ask if there is a reason why he/she has not been able to get his chores done. Perhaps small details such as end of day assignments are being forgotten or are not clear. The first thing you need to find out is if there is really a problem, or if you are the one who is mistaken. It would be frustrating to create a confrontation if you simply looked at the assignment list wrong, or if there was another list you did not see.

When answering this question, be cognizant of word selection. For example, you should utilize the word *discuss*, instead of *confront*. You are attempting to convey to the interviewer or interview board that you are assuming the positive. A harsh or condemning word such as *confront* will negate your positive outlook.

Now, think about the respect you'll earn if you address the problem privately and professionally (especially if there is an acceptable reason for the neglect), and the respect you could lose if you handled a simple situation poorly. Remember, the last thing a busy supervisor wants to hear is a complaint about somebody not doing his or her job, so aim to resolve it at the lowest level!

A word of caution here: As with *Situational* questions, if the interview board offers enough information to prove your fellow co-worker is blatantly disregarding his duties, you must pursue the issue up the chain of command to your supervisor. If the issue is unethical or poses a threat to any person's safety, this must also be pursued up the chain of command, no matter how high you need to take it.

Homework

List 15 interpersonal skills that you possess. Use a separate piece of paper, or write your notes in your Interview Rule Book Workbook.

Bizarre, Weird, or Just Different Questions

Examples of Bizarre questions:

How many cows are there in Canada? - Google Interview

If you were a pizza delivery person, how would you benefit from a pair of scissors? - Apple Interview

These types of questions have become popular by various large companies. From the research we have completed, there is no right or wrong answer. The objective of these types of questions is to see how creative you are in finding solutions, solving problems, or ideation. We recommend trying to come up with something creative while incorporating the TopScore Top5. The bottom line is to get creative and market yourself. There are many examples of these types of questions on the internet, so start coming up with some answers in your head so you are prepared for these peculiar questions.

Core Values, Skills & Abilities

Every field has core values and skillsets that are needed to do the job right and to stay on top of your game, as well as stories that lead up to why people need you. Here is one that we came up with as firefighters, the profession we happen to know best. Think about this in relation to the profession you want to get into and come up with your own based on that profession. Know your core values, and the core values required in your desired profession. Read our short story of why people search for us and what our core values are. The core values we chose to use should be core values for almost all professions. Use them as a springboard to come up with your own list of core values and stories. We phrased our core values in a very generic manner and you should be able to use these core values as your own. Do the homework on these key values to make them fit your own.

Core Values of Your Profession

Rule: Develop stories the interviewer or interviewing board will remember.

Question: "*What makes you or will make you successful as a [profession]?*"

Answer: They are faced with situations, which exceed their abilities to cope. Firefighters face a huge variety of challenges. You need a broad range of expertise to succeed. Firefighting requires an individual to think quickly on his or her feet and react promptly and correctly to situations, which astound the normal citizen. On any given shift at the firehouse, you may be called on to use your strength and knowledge to forcefully open the door of a structure engulfed in flame, use your chemistry skills to determine how to take care of a hazardous material spill, utilize your mechanical skills to fix a broken fire pump or tap into your interpersonal skills to console a grieving widow who has just witnessed her spouse pass from this world.

The saying, "Jack of All Trades" has been used to describe firefighters. We disagree, for unlike the second portion of the saying, "Master of None," a firefighter must be a master of them all. There is no room for error; your fellow citizens depend on you.

We provide some of the Core Values we believe are essential to becoming a successful firefighter and that need to be woven into your TopScore Top5 answers. There are many important Core Values, and yours can be different, but do keep these in mind and work on the ones that would apply to your profession.

Leadership

Leadership is the ability to positively influence others toward the achievement of a goal, and it is an important personality trait in many professions. Leaders exude self-confidence (not arrogance) and respect the thoughts and opinions of others. Strong leadership fosters teamwork. An outstanding leader creates an atmosphere that inspires others to achieve their full potential. Leaders will have a vision of excellence that motivates and provides encouragement. A leader who has demonstrated integrity creates a level of trust and confidence. Leading by example is the expectation of all firefighters as well as an expectation of many others in many other professions, especially when interacting with the public or within the community.

Most companies and businesses would rather promote from within the company, and leadership can be shown in your daily life as well as from the first day you are employed. If you are in a new job with other new employees, you can organize a meeting after work to discuss different things that each of you learned throughout the week. You can lead from any level in an organization. It is usually best to lead by example. Start a food drive, collect money for disaster relief, start a softball team. There are many ways to lead without being the boss.

From the first day, you'll need to be a good follower. You'll need to follow Standard Operating Procedures, employee handbooks and direct instructions from your superior. It is important to show the interviewer or board how you have been successful as a follower in previous jobs and life experiences, but, at the same time, you need to express your previous and current ability to lead.

Think about where and when you have displayed positive leadership skills, and write a list of five times you have displayed unique leadership skills.

Homework

Write out five ways you have demonstrated leadership. Use a separate piece of paper, or write your notes in your Interview Rule Book Workbook.

TEAMWORK

Every highly functioning company functions as a team. We encourage you to participate actively on teams with projects or on committees. Build respect from peers by contributing to the goals of the group. Model expected behaviors to accomplish team goals. Commit to the success of the group. Focus on the group's needs when taking action. Act professionally and demonstrate flexibility. Always consider the impact of your actions on the group.

Everyone has been part of a team at some point in their lives. Teamwork should be one of the strongest points you convey in an interview.

Think about where and when you have exhibited outstanding teamwork in your own life, and write a list of five times you have displayed this trait.

Homework

Write out five ways you have demonstrated teamwork. Use a separate piece of paper, or write your notes in your Interview Rule Book Workbook.

Communication Skills

Excellent communication skills include highly developed listening skills as well as verbal and writing skills. The ability to articulate a point or make a verbal argument is crucial, as is the ability to concisely and properly make a point in writing. You should actively listen and engage the person you are communicating with while utilizing open body language. Solicit feedback from peers and supervisors for ways to increase your communication skills.

The easiest part of communicating is talking. The hardest and most important part is listening. Most people, when acknowledging their ability to communicate, default to how they effectively communicated a point they wanted to make. One of the toughest communication components can be listening, and more importantly, listening to his or her shortcomings.

I remember one of my first jobs as a young teen. I worked with a few friends on a landscape crew. It was a job outside under the sun and I was getting paid to hang out with friends who were also on the landscape crew. After two weeks on the job, I was called into the boss's office for my first evaluation. I walked into the meeting expecting a good report. I showed up to work early, worked as hard as or harder than most and I never complained. He began the evaluation by letting me know the things I did well. He then said if I wanted to stay employed with him, I needed to eliminate the horsing around while on the clock with my friends. He also said that I needed to talk less and listen more.

I told him I would work on those things, but felt the pain of what I initially took as an insult. It was tough stuff to hear as a sixteen-year-old, but he was right. Sometimes being a good listener can be painful, especially if you feel you are being corrected. By taking his advice, however, I was better for it. Listening has become a new priority for me whenever I am coached by someone who speaks of my shortcomings.

Homework

Write out five ways you have demonstrated communication skills. Use a separate piece of paper, or write your notes in your Interview Rule Book Workbook.

Professional Development

Professional development is very important to most companies. To develop professionally, you should measure yourself against this checklist:

- ✓ Do I act professionally?
- ✓ Am I focused on the mission?
- ✓ Do I serve the customer to the best of my abilities?
- ✓ Do I treat everyone with respect?
- ✓ Do I display self-discipline?
- ✓ Do I demonstrate, model, and incorporate the tenets of trustworthiness, respect, responsibility, fairness, and caring?
- ✓ Do I learn, embrace, and market the company's vision statement and mission statement (usually available on the company's website)?
- ✓ Have I shown initiative?
- ✓ Do I pursue growth in every endeavor?
- ✓ Do I model a strong work ethic?
- ✓ Do I remain focused until a project is complete?
- ✓ Do I take responsibility for my actions?

When you measure yourself against this checklist, be honest. Most importantly, if you screw up, you need to own it. Everyone has messed up. Maybe the interviewer or someone on the interview board has had the same misfortune in life. It just might make for a connection with a board member or the interviewer.

Whatever you do, when faced with a failure or mistake from your past in an interview, **never lie**. Hold true to your word.

Professional development is continuous and is achieved in a variety of ways. This can be done with continuing education, seminars, podcasts, on the job experience and learning from people in the same field. Think about where and when you have improved or displayed positive professional development traits.

Homework

Write out five ways you have demonstrated personal development traits. Use a separate piece of paper, or write your notes in your Interview Rule Book Workbook.

Physical and Technical Expertise

Does your job require you to be in great shape with a high level of cardiovascular fitness? If the position you are interested in is at all physical in nature, begin a fitness program today. Your physical presence will make a strong impression to the interviewer or oral board when you walk through the door. You need to show the interviewer or the board that you are fit for duty now, and that you will be fit for duty twenty-five years from now. Employers seeking to hire for these types of positions are searching for someone who will have a lifestyle of physical fitness. If you have not started a fitness lifestyle and want to work in a position that calls for it, start working on it now.

Homework

Write out five ways you have displayed physical traits and abilities. Use a separate piece of paper, or write your notes in your Interview Rule Book Workbook.

Innovation

Innovators are not afraid of change, and are willing to consider a variety of alternatives as a solution to their problems. They possess the vision of where they would like to go and explore multiple options, which allows them to reach their desired destinations. At the same time, innovators understand the various impacts of change and strive to think through options carefully before acting.

One of the best opportunities a supervisor can give a subordinate is to empower them to complete a task using the subordinate's own solution. The supervisor describes how the result should look when complete. This gives the subordinate the freedom to be innovative in how the job is to be completed.

Homework

Write out five ways you have demonstrated innovation. Use a separate piece of paper, or write your notes in your Interview Rule Book Workbook.

Diversity

People who truly value diversity understand the contributions made by people of all nationalities, races, colors, sexual orientations, and political or religious ideologies. They understand the value of different viewpoints, and utilize conflict management skills to bring about dynamic results. Diversity is broader than those categories protected by law and include some substantial differences in lifestyle and personality. This is what makes us unique as human beings. Successful candidates are confident enough in their own beliefs to appreciate a different perspective or point of view.

Homework

Write out five ways you have embraced diversity. Use a separate piece of paper, or write your notes in your Interview Rule Book Workbook.

Customer Service Skills

Customer service is critical in any successful business. There are numerous businesses competing for the same customers in nearly all industries. Often, businesses gain customers through great customer service. Consider: If you are going to get a service or product from one company over the other in which the price is relatively the same, you will go with the one with the best customer service. Customer service is the backbone of business. It has the power to make or break a company. The needs of the customer take precedence over the needs of the person delivering the service. A person with customer service skills understands perception is as important as the service delivered.

Let's take a look at an example of good customer service:

I worked for a local grocery store during high school, and my employer prided himself on the store's high level of superior customer service. It was on the first page of the employee handbook. I remember reading a particular paragraph that stated:

> *"If it is good for the customer and falls in line with the core values of the store, then it is a win-win."*

One night, I was helping an elderly lady by bagging her groceries. I asked her if she minded me taking the groceries out to her car. She replied that she lived behind the store in a mobile home park, and would make a few trips walking back and forth using a cart she left by the front door of her house. I told her I wasn't going to let that happen and walked her cart and the groceries to her front door. This was one of those specific incidents that the employee handbook did not cover. I did follow-up through the chain of command to my immediate supervisor, and he was pleased with the decision. He added that he would support that type of customer service any day.

Homework

Write out five ways you have demonstrated excellent customer service. Use a separate piece of paper, or write your notes in your Interview Rule Book Workbook.

TopScore Marketing Priorities

Rule: Blend your Marketing Priorities with the TopScore Top5 for the best possible answer.

Rule: Make sure you have perfected the TopScore Top5 before you start adding the Marketing Priorities.

The Polish. Once you feel confident in your interviewing skills, you can start to tailor your answers. Your answers will align your attributes with the greatest needs of the particular business or company for which you are interviewing. These are your **Marketing Priorities.** If the business or company takes pride in their internal customer service with members working as one team with one direction, then you might have "team player" as one of the marketing priorities to communicate in your interview.

For your Marketing Priorities, make a list of your top twenty attributes. Use a separate piece of paper, or write your notes in your Interview Rule Book Workbook. These can be anything from a great sense of humor to a fierce loyalty to friends and family. This may seem like a large number, so brainstorm. Remember, there are no wrong ideas when you are brainstorming. Ask family and friends to assist you in this endeavor. Look at your Personal History from earlier in this book. Examples might include your education, work history, and awards. Some of these may be extremely obvious and may already be listed on your resume.

Once you have twenty items on your list, narrow it down to ten. Once again, utilize those closest to you to assist you in paring down the twenty to your top ten. These ten remaining items are your **TopScore Marketing Priorities.** They will be molded with the **Core Value** answers you listed previously and crafted into an answer utilizing the **TopScore Top5** structure. It will take practice, but once mastered, you will speak flawlessly when sitting before the interviewer or oral panel.

Here is an example of ten items as your **TopScore Marketing Priorities** for you to use as a guide. Tailor your list to meet your own Marketing Priorities for the position you are pursuing. Remember that your list of marketing priorities may change dramatically with the different types of jobs you interview for, and in some cases, it may not be possible to narrow it down exclusively to ten (we will discuss this later). ***Example: Computer Operator Job***

According to the job description, this position requires a person who is a 1) dependable 2) team member with 3) great communications skills. They need to be able to 4) make good decisions while solving problems. The company is looking for someone who is able to 5) plan, organize and prioritize work. They are able to 6) obtain and process information as needed to do the job, but can also 7) adapt to a constantly changing situation. The company is seeking someone who has 8) technical knowledge related to the job and is 9) proficient in computer software.

These traits are being demonstrated in the order that they are listed for ease of demonstration. Be aware that in an actual interview, they will probably not be in such order.

1. Dependability

I have always been described as being dependable. It goes back to what I was taught growing up-giving someone my word and sticking to it. If there is something that needs to be done, then I am your man/woman. My word is my bond.

2. Team player

I am a dedicated teammate. Sports have been a part of my life since I was six years old. I have played on teams that have gone undefeated as well as those that didn't win a single game. My memories when we finished last were of the fun we all had playing together, not of losing.

3. Ability to communicate.

I communicate with people both inside and outside the organization. There are people who reserve respect for the external customer and treat their co-workers without the same level of respect. You will not see any difference of my level of respect to either the internal customer or the external customer.

4. Decision Making and Problem Solving.

One of my greatest strengths is to think outside the box to solve problems, which gives me clarity when making decisions. One thing that I was taught early was a five-step process to solving problems:

1. Identify and define the problem.
2. Brainstorm potential solutions.
3. Evaluate solutions.
4. Implement a solution.
5. Evaluate Success.

5. Planning, organizing and prioritizing work.

Because I have always been a confident, quick learner, it did not take long for supervisors to pile work on me. A lot of this work required me to learn on the job and with little supervision. I had to come up with an organized plan and make certain the priorities were being met.

6. Obtaining and processing information.

As I mentioned, I am a fast learner. For me, obtaining and processing information quickly is two parts of a three-part system. The third and most critical part is capturing a full understanding of the information. Understanding informs my situational awareness.

7. Ability to adapt to changing situations.

I am adaptable to any given changing situation. I grew up in a broken household. My parents divorced when I was 10, and this started a windfall of change. At age 14, I moved from California, where I was living with my mom, to Boise, Idaho to live with my father. I had lived in the same town with the same friends my entire life, but despite that, I was able to meet and make new friends almost immediately. I adapted to the changing situation, and moreover, I thrived.

8. Technical knowledge related to the job.

I am already a student of the trade. It is my ambition to be an exceptional professional at this position. My desire and passion have me reading numerous publications and learning as much as I can. I obtained certifications (for example) in order to be more prepared when hired.

9. Proficiency with computer software programs.

I consider myself "Intermediate in Proficiency" when it comes to working with computer programs. I can work with sections, create templates, use styles and customize them. I can also create and format complex tables, manage table data, create mail merges, sort and filter them, customize toolbars and insert graphic elements.

Problem, Action, Result (PAR)

PAR's are a great way to share the successes you have had in life or at a previous job. These were times when you **identified a problem**, then **took action** on the problem and **positive results followed**. For example, let's say you worked in a kitchen for a local restaurant. Shortly after starting the job, you almost slipped on the floor near the fryer. Another employee told you that they had two different employees fall in that same location over the past two months and one of them had injured themselves. You then took it upon yourself and approached the kitchen manager with an idea to move a non-slip floor mat to the location in question. He ordered one, and since the day you placed it on the floor, there have been zero falls and zero slips.

Remember: Anytime you can demonstrate these traits the interview board with real stories, it makes it easier for them to make strong predictions of how you will be as an employee for them. Go the interview prepared, and do not miss out on these opportunities.

ORAL INTERVIEW WRAP UP

TopScore's Top5 is the foundation for each **Real** answer. The **TopScore Marketing Priorities** interwoven with the **Core Values** to serve as the polish used to ensure you've not only answered the question, but have provided the interviewer with enough information to really understand who you are and the value you bring. Be thoroughly prepared for the board or interviewer to close with a question such as:

"Is there anything you would like to add?"

One interviewer we consulted stated that they have never given a perfect score on an interview to a candidate who did not answer this question. Look at it as an opportunity to let the board know about one or two of your marketing priorities that you might have missed.

During your closing remarks, you should briefly touch on each of the following items. Don't delve too deeply into these items; your response should simply be a concise summary of what you have discussed during the interview:

- ✓ Summarize your qualifications.
- ✓ Emphasize one of your best marketing priorities.
- ✓ Reiterate how you would share the company's values.
- ✓ Illustrate how proud you will be to be a part of the company.
- ✓ Thank them for their time and inform them you look forward to working with them in the future.

THE PLUS OR MINUS OF YOUR INTERVIEW SCORE

Keep in mind that in addition to the answers you provide, , there are other key traits the interviewer is looking for. To ace the interview, you should:

- ✓ Speak Confidently.
- ✓ Be clear and concise.
- ✓ Be interested and engaging.
- ✓ Be Attentive.
- ✓ Be Articulate so that you are easy to follow.
- ✓ Be respectful to the board or interviewer and communicate in an appropriate tone.

Avoid the following missteps:

- ✓ Speaking incomplete thoughts.
- ✓ Rambling or make yourself hard to follow.
- ✓ Speaking so softly that the board has to ask you to speak louder.
- ✓ Being repetitive.
- ✓ Being over confident.
- ✓ Being unprofessionally casual.

THANK-YOU CARD

Rule: Write a thank-you card.

A thank-you card is one last opportunity to positively influence the interview board or interviewer. At this point, you've provided a professional resume and excelled at the interview by implementing the TopScore system. The interview board or interviewer will take a copy of your resume to assist them while they determine the rank and order of the interview pool. Think of the thank-you card as an opportunity to showcase your name and demonstrate your interest in becoming a member of their company.

Handwrite the thank-you card. A handwritten card demonstrates a desire to go above and beyond what the average candidate would do. Anybody can sit down for a few seconds and fire off a clean-looking email with the use of grammar and spell check, but few are willing to take the time to handwrite a thank-you card to each of the board member or to the interviewer. Ensure that you mail them in time for the interviewers to receive soon after the interview. In fact, we suggest you write the cards immediately after the interview and mail them either the same day or the following day at the latest.

You do not need to use this as an opportunity to remind the board members of why you would be a great hire. Your successful interview already answered that question. Your goal should simply be to thank them for their valuable time.

ADDITIONAL TOPSCORE RULES FOR THE ORAL INTERVIEW

These simple rules will allow you to make a positive first impression to the interviewer and gain their interest from the moment you walk into the room. Failing to follow these rules will significantly decrease your chances of gaining the job before the interview has even begun!

Rule: Be nice to everyone you meet, practice random acts of kindness and treat everyone with respect.

Obviously, we do this because it is our duty as fellow human beings. The ripple effect we receive from this type of behavior is immeasurable, and the best part is, you will feel better about yourself as a person as well. When you feel better about yourself, you will become more confident and happier. You never know: You may be speaking with someone who, years down the road, might be the one person who decides if you get a dream job you have applied for.

Not long ago I was in Big City Coffee, my favorite coffee shop in Boise, Idaho. I had my teenage daughter with me. I told my daughter that whenever she meets someone, to smile, show respect, and share her kindness. While standing in line at Big City the owner, whom I have known for the past 20 years approached me with a hug and a hello. I introduced the owner, Sarah, to my daughter. My daughter smiled at her and said, *"Nice to meet you,"* as she extended her hand for a shake.

Sarah immediately said, "How old are you?" Alexia, my daughter, replied that she was 16. Sarah asked for Alexia to send her a resume on the spot. Now, I can't prove that she would have been offered a job if she wasn't so respectful and polite, but I can say it surely didn't hurt!

Rule: Make certain you bring your best to every job you work.

When you start your first job, you begin to create your own work history. How important is your work history? It is the most legitimate place a potential employer can look to assess your skills and capabilities.

Rule: Never accept a job where you know you will not be motivated to give your best.

A mediocre performance in one job may cost you a future job, even a dream job. Job history will be the primary item that future employers thoroughly review to help them predict what kind of employee you will be.

Rule: Don't accept a job you cannot do.

With high hopes of my first newspaper route at age 11, I stuffed 50 newspapers in my pack and set off on my route. I didn't consider the weight of 50 newspapers on my 85-pound body. That job lasted one day but provided me a lesson that lasted a lifetime. When accepting a job, carefully consider the pay, position, willingness to relocate, working graveyard or non-traditional hours, and room for advancement.

Rule: Look the part.

When I was young I had a neighbor who worked as a waiter for a popular chain restaurant. At the time, my neighbor was in his early 20's and studying to become an actor. He was offered an audition along with twenty-five other people to read for a commercial spot for the restaurant. He ended up getting the role. He was the only person who showed up for the casting call wearing his work uniform: bib, uniform shirt and pants. He was dressed in restaurant attire, and he got the part.

It is critical that you dress according to the expectations and core values of the employer. I am not saying to go out and find the matching outfit or uniform of the company. What I do recommend is that if the grooming standard for a particular job says *"no beards or exposed tattoos,"* you may want to shave and cover up any exposed tattoos.

Rule: Stay Positive

Stay positive in your interview. Even if you are answering questions about a last job that you hated, list the great things you learned from it. Even in the most negative employment situations, you need to do your best to find the positive.

Rule: Eye contact

One of the biggest mistakes you can make in an interview is to look down at your cell phone while talking, or failing to make eye contact in the conversation. When you look down frequently throughout a conversation, it can lead the interviewer to believe that you are not trustworthy. Strong eye contact shows confidence, and confidence is a sign of leadership.

Rule: Clean up your Facebook and Twitter Accounts

It is not uncommon for prospective employers search the social media profiles of their candidates for any red flags. While most people tell you to watch every single thing you upload, there's a much easier solution. According to *Social Sweepster*, their app will detect and delete pictures of red solo cups, beer bottles, and other "suspicious" objects. It even detects profanity from your past posts!

"Too many recruiters reject candidates because of something they found on their social platforms" Social Sweepster CEO Tom McGrath says. "We help you create the first impression on your own terms."

Rule: Be enthusiastic

Nobody wants to spend 30 minutes listening to a humdrum monotone voice. Have some enthusiasm and engage the interviewer in the subject matter.

Rule: Smile as often as you can during the interview

Smiling is contagious. It makes people feel good. When you smile, it also shows the board or interviewer that you are enjoying yourself despite the stress the interview is causing

Rule: Shake hands

Your handshake must be firm, but not overpowering.

Rule: Show positive body language

Your body language accounts for an enormous amount of what you communicate. Be engaging. Recording your mock interviews will allow you to assess and correct any issues with your body language. Take a neutral body position. Sit as though a string were connecting your head to the ceiling. Leaning back or slouching in the chair is seen as lazy or arrogant, and leaning forward can be perceived as overly aggressive.

Rule: Lose the *um's*

If they are counting the number of times you say "*um,*" you will probably not get hired. If you set the record for "*um's*", you definitely won't get hired! Record your practice interviews and strive to eliminate them.

Rule: The ignore

If more than one person is interviewing you, try to make eye contact and try to engage each of them.

Rule: Positive statements

If the oral board asks how you feel about working with different and sometimes difficult types of people, assure them that you only think positively and make sure that your response reflects that concept. If they ask about your current or past jobs, only respond with a positive angle. If you don't have anything nice to say, just state that it was time for a change.

Rule: Never lie

Do not lie. They are on the interview board or are the interviewer because they are very good judges of character.

Rule: Keep your phone on silent

Make sure you phone is on silent mode, whether you are stopping by for an application or going in for the interview itself. This will eliminate any possible interruptions of your phone playing some lame ringtone and will keep you from appearing to be rude.

Rule: During your interview, keep your phone powered off

However, keep it available to be able to check your schedule for a follow up if needed.

Rule: Do not chew gum

This should go without saying, but it would not be here unless we had heard multiple horror stories from interviewers.

Rule: Do not interrupt anyone

This includes talking over someone.

Rule: Research the company

Know the company and problems they have and how you can help. Know the direction the company is going. Know the industry including their competition.

Rule: Show interest when the interviewer is talking

Maintain perfect eye contact with body language that conveys you being 100 percent dedicated to hearing them speak.

Rule: Remember the interviewer's name and use it

Rule: Be aware that some questions should not be asked during an interview

Learn what questions the interview board should not ask. You need to find a way to answer or respond to illegal questions. Examples of questions that should not be asked include any questions that reveal your age, race, national origin, gender, religion, marital status, and sexual orientation.

Rule: Do research on the going rate of pay

Do research on the pay and benefits are in your area for the position for which you are applying. Know what you are willing to take and what you would want.

Rule: Show up thirty minutes early for your interview

If they are ahead of schedule, your effort will be noticed and appreciated.

Rule: Prepare for a background investigation

If there is any possibility that the position you are interested in may require a background check, get all of your background items collected before you need them.

Some background checks involve many pages of information, and you will usually have one week to collect everything. If you have moved out of state from where you went to high school and college, this will make it difficult to acquire your transcripts in time. Keep in mind that some background checks can go back ten years or more. Do the work beforehand. This info will also be helpful in filling out your application.

Rule: Application

Get your application into the employer in a timely fashion. Take the time to have someone proofread it. Even if you are an English major and the world spelling bee champion four years in a row, have a friend or family member double check your work. Even if the application is all online, someone should still look at it before you push the submit button.

Rule: Thank-you letter

A nice (preferably hand-written) thank-you letter is greatly appreciated. It also looks professional and gives you another chance for the company to see your name. Don't forget: it is a thank-you letter; therefore, you are not going to talk about yourself.

KEYWORDS

Rule: Use keywords! Your interviewers will notice.

Below are keywords you should know and utilize in an interview. We've included a few examples, but do your research and discover more that are relevant to the particular industry for which you are applying. These definitions are from *Merriam-Webster*'s *Dictionary*,

Wikipedia, and *Dictionary.com,* as well as TopScore preference when applied within the scope of the fire service. They will help you present yourself as the true professional you are.

Pride: A high or inordinate opinion of one's own importance, dignity, merit or superiority, as cherished in the mind or as displayed in bearing and conduct.

Respect: Esteem for or a sense of the worth or excellence of a person; a personal quality or ability or something considered as a manifestation of a personal quality or ability.

Integrity: Consistency of principles, actions, values, methods, and measures. Depth and breadth of a value system may also be significant factors due to their congruence with a wider range of observations. People have integrity to the extent that they behave according to the values, beliefs and principles they claim to hold. One's value system may evolve over time while retaining integrity if inconsistencies are accounted for and resolved. Hypocrisy results when one part of a value system is demonstrably at odds with another, and the person or group of people holding those values fails to account for the discrepancy. Hypocrisy is the opposite of integrity.

Dedication: A feeling of very strong support for or loyalty to someone or something.

Excellence: The state or quality of excelling, particularly in the field of business and organization. Excellence is considered an important value and a goal to be pursued.

Leadership: The position or function of a leader, a person who guides or directs a group.

Accountability: In leadership roles, accountability is the acknowledgment and assumption of responsibility for actions, products, decisions and policies including the administration, governance and implementation within the scope of the role or employment position. This encompasses the obligation to report, explain, and be answerable for resulting consequences.

Responsibility: The state or fact of being responsible, answerable or accountable for something within one's power, control or management.

Chain of Command: A series of administrative or military ranks, positions, etc., in which each has direct authority over the one immediately below.

Camaraderie: A spirit of familiarity and trust existing between friends.

Tolerance: A fair, objective, and permissive attitude toward those whose opinions, practices, race, religion, nationality, etc., differ from one's own. Freedom from bigotry.

Loyalty: Faithful to one's oath, commitments or obligations.

Fair: Free from bias, dishonesty or injustice.

Flexibility: A personality trait; the extent to which a person can cope with changes in circumstances and think about problems and tasks in novel, creative ways. This trait is used when stressors or unexpected events occur, requiring a person to change his or her stance, outlook or commitment.

Reliability: Consistently good in quality or performance; able to be trusted.

Honesty: Being able to be trusted for one's word.

Motivation: Interest in or enthusiasm for doing something.

Positive Attitude: Displaying a positive state of mind or feeling. I want to see this as an entire chapter under preparing for the interview/promotion etc.

Professionalism: The level of excellence or competence expected from a professional.

Team Oriented: Team oriented means you don't think of just yourself. You include others in your decisions. Everyone has a contributing factor in the operations and decisions.

Trust: Firm reliance on the integrity, ability or character of another person.

Selfless Service: Putting the needs of others before one's own.

Compassion: Deep awareness of the suffering of another coupled with the wish to relieve it.

Attitude: The manner in which someone carries oneself.

Respect: Showing admiration for someone based on his or her abilities, qualities or achievements.

Responsibility/Accountability: A form of trustworthiness; the trait of being answerable to someone for something or being responsible for one's conduct.

Excellence: A state of possessing good qualities to an eminent degree; exalted merit; superiority in virtue.

Empowerment: Knowledge of and faith in one's own ability.

Humility: Freedom from arrogance.

Success: The achievement of something desired, planned or attempted.

Exceed: To be better than. Go beyond what is expected.

Mentor: An influential counselor, coach or leader

Excel: Being exceptionally good and proficient in a subject or talent

Sample Real Questions

Below are a series of sample questions to help you practice the concepts you've learned in this book. Some might seem unusual, but your focus should be on connecting these questions to your desired industry.

Who is your favorite past U.S. President and why? This is a perfect question to help you use your keywords. Pick five good keywords and match them with a president.

What is the most important invention of all time, and why? Use this one to demonstrate your company knowledge. Pick an invention and relate it to what you know about the department. Take the wheel, for example. Talk about how the company benefits from the invention of the wheel. You can then transition to your department knowledge.

Why is it important to be dependable? Dependability shows dedication and it can carry over through an entire team. Dependability makes people passionate, and it makes people work hard for each other. It can be contagious within an organization. Being dependable begets trust from your teammates, community, and supervisors. It shows your dedication to obtain a goal and shows self-sacrifice.

What word would best describe you? Look at the company's mission statement and core values.

What is the most appealing aspect of working for our company? You will need to figure this out. Look at the mission statement and keywords.

How could you help maintain good relationships around the office? Be nice and show interest in your fellow co-workers' families and hobbies.

What are three characteristics of a good employee? Look at the department's mission statement and core values and let them know which ones you have.

What type of person would you find most difficult to work with? Think of safety and gear your answer around that.

What do you know about the organizational structure of this company? Know that most departments have the following divisions: Administration Division, Operations Division, Training Division and Logistics Division.

Give some examples of how you provide customer service in your current job.

What is the primary goal of this company? Start with customer service!

What do you think of your previous boss? Remember to only use positive statements.

What motivates you? This is another great question that allows you to implement those keywords we referenced earlier!

Give an example of when you worked with someone different than you. Remember, you need to keep your responses positive.

Would you ever disobey an order? Yes, if it has to do with my safety or the safety of others.

Define sexual harassment and give your feelings about the subject. Think about this before your interview.

What have you done to prepare for this position? I like to think that everything I have done in life so far has helped me prepare for this position.

What are you bringing to the job? If you're feeling stuck, go back and review your **TopScore Top5** lists!

Why would we select you over other candidates? This is a good question for using company knowledge and keywords.

Why do you want to work for this agency?

What do you know about this agency?

What are your strengths? Find out what their company values are. They could include customer service, fitness, tradition and many other things.

What are your weaknesses? Have a weakness that will not keep you from being hired, but that will allow you to show that you are working to improve yourself. Do not have a weakness that is really a strength. The interviewer will see right through it.

What would your previous employer say about you?

What word would best describe you?

What is the least appealing aspect of this career? Every job has a few flaws that people find frustrating. Find one but have a solution for it.

What do you think the future holds for this company?

When and how did you fail in a job or assignment? Admit your mistakes, but focus on what you learned from the experience.

What makes you think that you will be able to deal with the stress and strains of this job?

What is the advantage of working in teams?

What is the disadvantage of working in teams?

How do you handle conflict?

Describe a time when you disagreed with a coworker?

Describe a time you were asked to do something wrong?

What is the toughest decision you have ever had to make?

What does leadership mean to you? Give examples.

Why is a healthy lifestyle important to this company?

What does integrity mean to you? How do you practice it?

What is your biggest mistake in life?

How do you evaluate success?

Why are you leaving your current job?

What are the attributes of a good employee? What is the most important to you?

Where do you see yourself in five years? Ten years?

Describe a difficult problem you had to overcome.

How would your friends describe you?

Who has inspired you in life?

How would you handle racist/sexist comments?

Why do you want to work for this company? You would be surprised how many people do not have an answer for this question! Make sure you have a professional answer.

Sample What If Questions

What if you suspect a fellow coworker has a drug problem?

What if you see two coworkers exchanging answers on a test?

What if your boss clearly treats you unfairly, giving you much more work than he or she give to your coworkers?

What if you feel a fellow employee is not pulling his or her weight?

What if you are assigned a task that you strongly feel is unsafe?

FILLING IN YOUR OWN SCORECARD AND SCORESHEET

Now that you understand the TopScore process and are capable of crafting quality answers using the system, you need to understand the five categories typically used to grade an interviewee within most industries. These five categories are Leadership, Interpersonal Sensitivity, Cultural Diversity, Oral Communication, Problem Solving and Reasoning. The TopScore Interview scoring sheet is a measuring tool to see how well you perform in the interview setting within these five categories. A scorecard is an evaluation of your answers.

One of the biggest challenges we have identified with those preparing for an interview is failing to recognize what the oral board or interviewer is evaluating. For example, let's examine how one of our young daughters prepares for her gymnastics competitions, and, more importantly, how she prepares to be judged.

Rob Christensen has a 6-year old daughter who understands that the gymnastics judges will award her more points if her cartwheel is completed with straight legs. This item is important enough to warrant a specific block on the judge's score sheet. From the first day she learned a cartwheel, the importance of having straight legs was instilled in her mind, so much so that when she cartwheels around the house, she looks for feedback on the straightness of her legs. You need to maintain this same frame of mind when preparing for your interview. You need to understand what is on the interviewer's score sheet, and ensure you check every block for each question. It should be your goal to make it effortless for the interviewer to award you the maximum score for your interview.

TopScore Interview Score Sheet

Leadership

Synopsis: Motivates others to take desired action or adopt attitudes having a positive effect on behavior: guides a group with common tasks or goals towards task/goal accomplishment; commands attention and respect, shows an air of confidence; originates action and attempts to influence events to achieve goals; sets task objectives and priorities and establishes a course of action for self and/or others to accomplish a specific goal.

Excellent Leadership Skills: 90 to 100

Good Leadership Skills: 80 to 90

Acceptable Leadership Skills: 70 to 80

Poor Leadership Skills: 60 to 70

Interpersonal Sensitivity

Synopsis: Interacts with others to bring about desired attitudes; promotes cooperative relationships; is receptive to the suggestions of others; takes actions which indicates a consideration for the feelings and needs of others; shows an awareness of the impact that one's own behavior has on others.

Excellent Leadership Skills: 90 to 100

Good Leadership Skills: 80 to 90

Acceptable Leadership Skills: 70 to 80

Poor Leadership Skills: 60 to 70

Cultural Diversity

Synopsis: Understands other cultures and cultural values and is confident in working with others of different backgrounds and diversity. Can identify with the feelings, thoughts and behaviors of individuals from different cultural backgrounds. (A high score indicates that you are extremely capable of functioning in a culturally diverse workforce.)

Excellent Leadership Skills: 90 to 100

Good Leadership Skills: 80 to 90

Acceptable Leadership Skills: 70 to 80

Poor Leadership Skills: 60 to 70

Oral Communication

Synopsis: Oral communication conveys ideas or directives accurately, clearly and to the point; speaks smoothly and fluently, positively and enthusiastically; uses gestures, posture and eye contact with enhanced oral expression; is convincing and easy to understand; listens well to what others have to say.

Excellent Leadership Skills: 90 to 100

Good Leadership Skills: 80 to 90

Acceptable Leadership Skills: 70 to 80

Poor Leadership Skills: 60 to 70

Problem Solving and Reasoning

Synopsis: The ability to solve problems and make decisions is beneficial to any employer. When answering your questions, it is important to demonstrate your capability to address a variety of problems and explain how your reasoning leads to a successful solution.

Ability to remember details and recall facts, to identify problems, recognize signs or symptoms of a larger or broader problem, plan an appropriate plan of action to reach an objective, develop alternative solutions and evaluate their relative value, to make sound decisions on the spot, etc.

Excellent Leadership Skills: 90 to 100

Good Leadership Skills: 80 to 90

Acceptable Leadership Skills: 70 to 80

Poor Leadership Skills: 60 to 70

MOCK ORAL INTERVIEW PRACTICE

Directions

This scorecard is intended to be used by the person who is giving you a mock interview. The interviewer is to make note of the following: date, total time of the interview, time of each question answered, the interviewee's body language, fidgeting and "um's", eye contact, and clarity of speech.

The rating will be scaled from 1-10 with 10 being the highest score. The interviewer will mark from 1-5 the number of Personal History, Personal Stories, Keywords, and Company Knowledge communicated. It is recommended that you videotape the practice session. This form is to be utilized for every question asked.

Interview Rule Book Workbook contains extra scorecards, and you can also copy more if necessary.

TopScore Mock Interview Practice Scorecard

Interviewer(s): ________________

Question:

____

____

____?

Body Language___ Speech____ Eye Contact____
Time_____

Did the question get answered? Yes
No

Personal History Yes
No 1 2 3 4 5

Personal Story Yes
No 1

Company Knowledge Yes
No 1 2 3 4 5

Key Words Yes
No 1 2 3 4 5

NOTES:

____

____

____

____

____

____

WWW.INTERVIEWRULEBOOK.COM

TopScore Mock Interview Practice Review

After learning the TopScore system, you must practice the implementation of the system. We are huge proponents of the mock oral interview. These mock interviews can be done with family or friends. If you happen know someone you trust who is currently working in the field in which you are applying, ask them.

Regardless of where your mock interview is done, take it seriously and prepare to deliver your very best. We recommend you do at least four mock interviews within two weeks of reading this book. This will allow you to become comfortable with the skills you've learned and hone your presentation with a live audience. We also suggest that you video record your mock interviews using your cell phone or other device. This will provide you a frank assessment of your interviewing skills and will allow you to identify areas where you can improve.

When reviewing your mock interview, count each non-verbal pause. Count how many times you fill a void in the conversation with unnecessary words such as "*um*". Using "*um*" provides a chance for your brain to catch up with what you are trying to say. If you use "*um*" frequently, you need to find a way to stop. The board will not interrupt you because of a three second pause. It is better to use this strategy than to rely on *"um."*

Stay away from repeated phrases such as *like*. They will make you sound immature and unprofessional. For example,

> *"Like this one time, we like went to.."*

Also avoid repeating *"you know"* after a sentence. If you have this habit in your daily communications, fix it immediately. If you do not work on it now, it will come out during your interview without you even recognizing it.

ASKING FOR A RAISE OR PROMOTION WITH THE TOPSCORE TOP5

When pursuing a raise or a promotion within your company, approach it no differently than you would an interview question. Start building your pitch while utilizing the **TopScore Top5**.

The main question you will encounter when seeking a raise is:

"What makes you feel you should get a raise?"

Talk about the different 'hats' that you have successfully worn within the company and opportunities in which you truly made a difference in the company at your working level. Focus on those PARs (problem, action, results) that demonstrate how you have been instrumental in within the company. Pick one particular story that shows off your worth as an employee. Do this confidently, but avoid appearing arrogant. For some, it can be very uncomfortable to speak of their personal victories as an employee, but you will need to overcome this in order to earn that raise or promotion.

Rule: Don't blind-side your supervisor when asking for a raise. Give him/her a heads up. Send an email stating something like:

> *"I'm hoping we can sit down, and I'd like to make the case to you for revisiting my salary."*

Rule: Do not throw coworkers under the bus to make yourself look better.

Rule: The reason for the raise should always be tied to the worth you are bringing to the company. The reason should not be because you are broke.

When asking for a raise, be sure to use the TopScore system. Include **Keywords, Personal History** and **Company Knowledge**. Use keywords that are popular with your company, and be sure to include parts of your company motto and vision statement. Personal History will include things that you have done for the company that your boss knows about and additional things that he might not know that you have accomplished. Also, include things from your personal life that support your request for a raise.

For Company Knowledge, even if you have been at a company for 20 years, make sure you do some detailed research on the organization. Do research on how the company was founded. How did the founder get the idea, the money, and their initial vision? Where is the company today, and what your competitors are doing? Your research may even uncover things that your boss didn't know about the company. Things like this will show your boss that you really know and care about the company. Personal Stories should support your position. If your raise will include more responsibility, your stories should demonstrate how you have been able to handle similar adjustments in the past.

Just like your initial interview, it is imperative to practice and be prepared for any questions that may be headed your way

Rule: Know your value and the reasons *why* you should you should be given a raise. Look at parity of others performing the same work as well as cost of living adjustments.

Rule: A good time to ask for a raise is prior to budget planning for the upcoming fiscal year. Remember that the company you work for operates under a strict budget. If your boss is not in the position to offer a raise right now, discuss when might be a better time, and what you can do to better position yourself for that raise in the future. Finish the interview with a positive statement regarding if you do not get the raise. For example:

> *"I will continue to bring my 'A' game as I have from day one with this company but it never hurts to ask. Thank you for your time."*

Promotional Interview

A promotional interview will take on different approach. A current employee that has been with a company will not need to use "personal history" or "personal stories" that happen prior their current employment unless, of course, it is top marketable priority.

Rule: When using "Personal History" or "Personal Stories," try to stay within your WORK history of the company *unless* it is a marketable priority from a previous position outside the company that supports your candidacy for the promotion.

Rule: Tell the supervisor your plans and goals for position once it's yours. Talk about how the company will benefit from your promotion. Make it easy for them to predict your future success based off of your previous successes.

YOUR RESUME AND THE ROAD TO SUCCESS

Your resume is an important piece of the interview process. After you leave a lasting impression on the interview board or interviewer by implementing the TopScore system, your resume is the tangible piece they take with them. The application you may have filled out will most likely be a basic form without much detail.

The resume is an important marketing piece for you, and you should treat it as such. Your resume should be kept to one page. Be sure to use high quality paper. A cover letter will not be needed when directly handing out your resume, but be prepared in case one is requested.

Below are the general rules for a resume. Resume templates are available for free over the internet. They will provide numerous layouts to choose from and even have suggestions for various job types.

Resume Tip: When including a list of personal references on your resume, include a small excerpt from their reference letter if they wrote you one. For example, one of your personal references may be John Doe.

> ***John Doe*** ***Previous Supervisor at ABC Store***
> ***Phone # 555-1212***
> *"In all my years of supervision, I have yet to find anyone else that I could rely on for the most difficult assignments as well as Jane." - John Doe*

This lets your character references speak through your resume as indirect marketing. When you utilize this practice, you will help resume stand out by letting your great references resonate with the hiring committee.

Rule: We recommend getting your resume done right the first time. There are classes and software if you do not want to pay a professional. This is not a time to cut corners.

Rule: Have a quality resume on good paper and a cover letter that is proper for your industry. We also recommend you put some of your hobbies in your resume or cover letter if it is appropriate. Anything that could help the interviewer remember you. This information may peak their interest and open the door to a memorable conversation during the interview.

MAKING THE TOPSCORE TOP5 WORK FOR YOUR BUSINESS TYPE

There are many different types of businesses, but to be concise, we are going to lump them all into two categories/interview types. They each have different hiring and interviewing practices that we must adapt to. Their interviewing practices may not always be ideal for the **TopScore Top5**, but through our system, you'll still walk in the room with an air of confidence and stand out from the competition. Statistically, your competition is generally walking in the interview with no preparation whatsoever. You will have what it takes to win the day and the job!

Let's learn about these two business types and how to approach their interview process:

TYPE ONE: GOVERNMENT OR LARGE BUSINESSES

We look at this type of job as a "traditional" job. This is when you are preparing for a position in which there is a definite job description within a definite agency, company, or department. In these situations, there is usually a considerable wait from the time you place your application to the time you will be called for your interview. This would be the case for governmental or state level jobs including fire or police jobs, anything within the federal or state government, or large businesses akin to railroads or hospitals. A good way to determine whether you may be applying for one of these jobs is that the job will have a definite *"job closing"* date or a *"job will be filled by"* date. These dates may be months in the future.

For these competitive interviews, it is not uncommon for interviewees to spend 50 hours in preparation of their interview using the TopScore system. Regardless of the different jobs you may be interviewing for, the preparation process is very similar. The key will be to always be prepared.

- ✓ Review and update your resume.
- ✓ Have a professional interview outfit cleaned, pressed, and hanging in your closet.

Rule: 6 months prior or as soon as the job is announced:

- ✓ Start doing research on the company or organization.
- ✓ Review your resume.
- ✓ Gather all background information.
- ✓ Spend one hour per week on learning your field's current events.
- ✓ Do one mock interview leading up to the true interview. Provide the interviewer of the mock interview with a list of TopScore's common interview questions and have them grade you according to the **TopScore Interview Score Sheet** utilizing the TopScore Scorecard. Do not take any timeouts if you stumble; learn to work yourself out of any mistakes you may make.
- ✓ Do one casual interview per month. This can be done on your own, answering questions into a video recorder, or with a friend or family member.

Rule: 3 months prior: Do a job shadow with the company. Start working in the information that you receive from the job shadow into your answers.

Rule: 1 month prior: Time to refresh your Company Knowledge! Do a mock oral and casual interview.

Rule: 1 week prior: Make sure you have your closing statement ready. Do two casual interviews and one last mock oral interview.

Rule: No coffee the day of the interview. You will be nervous enough during the interview. There is no need to make it worse by drinking a bunch of caffeine.

Rule: 1 hour prior: Be there early!

Rule: 2 minutes prior: Power pose! Maintain your TopScore Top5 confidence and enthusiasm. You've got this!

Type Two: Today's Fast Paced, Always Changing Job Market

Most of us are not going to have the leisure of knowing the exact job and business we are going to interview for three to six months in advance. In the current market, a person can apply for multiple jobs with numerous job descriptions depending on their industry.

For example, let's say a person graduates with an English degree with the intention of becoming a professional writer. It sounds simple, but there are probably hundreds of different directions this person could follow in pursuit of a career in writing. They could write articles, write for social media, become a journalist, a ghostwriter, an academic writer, a grant writer, or a novelist, just to name a few. All are very different and all qualify as "writing positions."

When this person wants a job, are they going to limit themselves to just one of these types of jobs? Probably not. They can't afford to. They need to work and start somewhere in their field. They are going to apply to many different opportunities and cross their fingers that they are called back on a few of them. If they **are** called back on a few of them, they have a few days, maybe a week to prepare for that interview.

How can the **TopScore Top5** be used in this type of situation? This situation is obviously not ideal, but it can still be used to make this person the best candidate for the job.

Rule: Adjust your resume and cover letter to the job description

When applying for these types of jobs, use your resume and cover letter as a fluid document, one that is always a work in progress. Read the job description and requirements carefully. Then, adjust your resume and cover letter to match your experience and qualifications to the specific job as well as you can. We understand that you may be applying for many jobs, but keep the job descriptions for each application. If you are called for the job, you can use the individual announcement to prepare for the interview.

Rule: Prepare for the interview

You may be asking yourself: "How can I prepare for a job interview when all of the jobs that I am applying for are different? I am applying to far too many jobs to prepare for each interview individually, particularly when I have no idea which ones I might be called back on, and I'll only have a few days to prepare!"

You would be surprised how similar many of these interviews will be. Look at your field and all of the jobs that you could possibly qualify for. What do they have in common? What qualities would a supervisor need in a candidate for these jobs? Teamwork? Organizational skills? Leadership skills? Look at the section in this book of the skills at the top traits that employers want their employees to have. Use that list and build upon it. We also recommend using the *Interview Rule Book Workbook*. Brainstorm from your personal experiences and stories. You may not be able to hit on everything, but you can properly prepare and ace that interview.

Rule: Practice interviewing

Even though you won't be able to use information about the particular job or focus on Company Knowledge just yet, you can still practice interviewing. Practice your keywords, personal story, and personal history firmly in place. Remember, most businesses are going to use very similar keywords: accountability, responsibility, loyalty and so on. Use the keywords given in this book as a launching point, and throw in any other keywords you can from your field.

Rule: Practice some more

You don't know when you're going to be called on an interview. Answer at least one or two questions from a mock or casual interview per week. You need to stay sharp and prepared for the real thing.

Rule: Crunch time

You've just gotten a call for an interview. It's next Tuesday, less than a week away. Luckily, 60 percent of your interview is already in the bag. Focus on job specifics and Company Knowledge. Review the job description thoroughly.

Is there anything specific to the job mentioned in that piece of paper that needs to be added to your presentation? Then, go online and do your research on the company. What is the company motto? Do they have anything interesting in their story? Spend your last several days getting down the specifics of the particular job and the company knowledge.

Rule: One question a day

Spend the last several days answering one question per day, putting in as much of the specific job knowledge and company knowledge as you can. More important than the company knowledge is eliminating your trepidation about answering the interview questions. Make sure that the knowledge that you can impart lacks the "*um's*" and frequent lengthy pauses. Even though your knowledge may not be as good as it could be, remember self-assurance and confidence can go a long way. Also, spend this time making sure your closing statement is ready to go.

Rule: No coffee the day of the interview

You will be nervous enough during the interview. There is no need to make it worse by drinking a bunch of caffeine.

Rule: Be there early!

Rule: Power pose

Maintain your confidence and enthusiasm. You've got this!

After the Interview for Either Type of Business

One of the best and fastest methods for learning from your interviews is to utilize the voice recorder on your cell phone as soon as you can after the interview. After the interview, you can listen to it so you can explore areas in which you can improve. At the very least, have a pen and paper to write down the information you remember from your interview.

Rule: Immediately after your interview, document the following:

- ✓ Names of members serving on the interview board or the name of the interviewer.
- ✓ All of the questions that you were asked.
- ✓ Your response to the questions.
- ✓ **TopScore Top5** utilization.
- ✓ What did you learn? From the board? About the process? About yourself?
- ✓ What should you have done differently?
- ✓ Send thank-you cards.

Rule: Be passionate and stay committed

CONGRATULATIONS!

You are now one-step closer to achieving your goal. Now comes the hard part. Practice.

We now want you to write out your answers to all the real questions listed above. Do as we did and put (PH) (PS) (KW) (CK) before each corresponding word or story, and then count them. If you have met the requirements, most likely, you have a complete and professional answer.

Once you have the **TopScore Top5** down, practice adding in your **Core Values** and **Marketing Priorities**. Don't worry about frequent practice making you sound 'canned'. You will not be able to remember these answers word for word, but you will have a pool of qualified ideas to draw from for that great answer.

We feel this book is that boost you need for success on your next job interview. We also know the value of one-on-one personal coaching. With personal coaching, we are able to make sure you are implementing our system correctly and answer any questions you have on the testing process. To sign up for one-on-one coaching, please visit our website at http://www.interview911.com/www.interviewrulebook.com

Thank you and good luck!

---

[i] Goleman, Daniel, "What Makes a Leader", Best of Harvard Business Review, 1998

Made in the USA
Middletown, DE
22 April 2017